Shoot Deer

A Guide to Hunting Whitetails

By Timothy McMahon

With thanks to Laura Bohn for the cover art.

I am writing this book with the goal of informing whitetail deer hunters on how to hunt whitetail deer. If you read every page of this book, then you should be able to go deer hunting and know what it is that you are supposed to do, where you are supposed to do it, and what you are supposed to do it with.

My qualifications for writing this book are fifteen years of hunting whitetail deer. During this time I have usually hunted more than 2 days a week, nearly every week, from the end of September through the first week of December. So far I have shot twenty-seven bucks, two does, and one buck fawn. I have shot them with compound bows, rifles, muzzleloaders, and I missed two bucks with a recurve bow. I started letting all 1 ½ year old bucks go when I was 17, a few years later I started letting 2 ½ year olds go and holding out for bigger bucks. During the 2012 Wisconsin early bow season, I let go 47 bucks before shooting one. My biggest buck was shot on the opening day of the 2008 Wisconsin firearms season, and its gross B&C score was 164 and change.

I am not claiming to be a great hunter, only a hunter who has spent lots of time in the woods and has been somewhat successful in shooting bucks.

My experience hunting deer has been primarily on several different properties in central Wisconsin, although I have also spent time in Northern Wisconsin. When I mention a month or a date or a season, you should understand that that date is appropriate for central Wisconsin and not for other places. It gets cold in Wisconsin in the winter and warm in the summer; things are different in the southern United States where it is much warmer, and deer activity occurs later in the year than it does in the north.

There are a variety of deer hunting methods. Most of my experience has been stand hunting. I will outline the general idea for all of the methods, but will spend the most time on the method that I know best. This method also happens to be the one used by most professional deer hunting writers and TV hosts...for a reason.

Do take note of whatever hunting laws exist in your area; I'd appreciate it if none of you do what I say and then get caught breaking the law because your laws are different from the ones that I am familiar with.

Hunting deer should not be dangerous if you take reasonable safety measures, such as not falling asleep while in a treestand. There is, though, one significant danger that hunters will face out in the woods. Deer ticks carry Lyme disease. Lyme disease is an awful incapacitating, for life, disease that you can get from deer ticks. Anytime that you return from the woods you need to check for any ticks. The bigger wood ticks, about 1/8", are not good, but they are not known to carry any awful diseases. The smaller, 1/16" deer tick can carry Lyme disease, and other diseases. If you are bit by a tick, then you need to go to the doctor right away and tell him that you need the prescription that treats Lyme disease. It can be prevented early. Be sure to say "Lyme disease", because I have heard of several people getting tick bites in the Midwest and then traveling to, say, Arizona and the doctors there may not be at all familiar with this disease. Symptoms are sore joints and a red bulls eye around the bite location.

And finally, this book is to help deer hunters to shoot as many of the biggest bucks that you are legally able to. Some hunters prefer to do some things in a less than efficient way. Some want to do things more traditionally, and shoot recurve bows and old muzzleloaders rather than the more efficient compound bows and rifles. I am not here to criticize their decision to do things the way they want, but I am going to write how to shoot as many bucks as possible, as efficiently as possible. My personal goal, when hunting, is to shoot as many of the biggest bucks that I am legally allowed. It is hard enough with the most advanced tools and methods; I don't feel the need to make it more difficult.

Table of Contents

1
Who? What? When? Where? How?

Why? Who? What? When? Where? How? These are the questions that we may ask before beginning a new venture. Let's look at "what" first.

What deer hunters are after is usually the whitetail deer. This is the most popular big game animal in North America. The whitetail deer is a large mammal that lives in most of North America, Central America, and in parts of Venezuela and Columbia.

A deer has four legs that end in hooves, a short tail, long ears, is brown except for the white belly and throat, and the male deer grows antlers every spring and sheds them each winter.

Why we deer hunters hunt varies by the hunter. Some of us want fresh wild meat. Some of us collect antlers. Some of us enjoy spending time in the woods. Some of us enjoy the company of our fellow hunters. And some of us like all of those things.

When we hunt deer is largely dependent on the hunting laws where we hunt. One of the great advantages of those who hunt professionally is that they travel across the country to hunt the deer season in several states, whose hunting seasons occur at different times. They get to hunt several seasons in one, where those of us who hunt for a hobby are generally stuck with the one hunting season of our own state.

The laws allow deer hunting in the fall and winter. In Wisconsin the deer season starts in late September and lasts through the first few days of January. In the South the season starts later, and ends later because the winters are not as cold and harsh in the South and deer activity is timed accordingly later.

Who hunts deer is also largely based on the laws of your hunting location. One may be six or eight and accompany a parent, or one may be twelve or thirteen and hunt on your own. There are licenses that are required by law and not everyone may be allowed to buy one. Check your local laws.

Many start young and hunt until they are old and unable. Some start because their father hunts and some hunt because their friends or spouse does. Deer hunters are mostly men, but more women hunt deer now, and there are all sorts of hunting equipment designed specifically for female hunters. I would advise you female hunters to buy the hunting equipment that you think is best, rather than whatever happens to be designed for girls.

If you can walk a mile, climb up and down a ladder and then walk that mile back without difficulty, then you are in good enough shape to do the majority of deer hunting activities. I find dragging deer that weigh more than I do to be the most physically demanding part of hunting, and a good problem to have. Being in better shape will help, of course, but is not absolutely necessary.

Where you hunt deer will greatly affect how you hunt deer. You might own your own land. You might hunt public land. You might lease land, or ask permission from the landowner. You may belong to a club that owns land. You might even travel to game farms and hunt there. For the most part, whitetail deer live to the east of the Rocky Mountains, from Mexico into southern Canada. They live in the woods, in backyards, and they live everywhere in between.

How you hunt deer will largely depend on where you hunt. Some land types are more suited for one type of hunt than others. The various strategies for hunting deer are: stand hunting, spot and stalk, driving, trailing, and hunting with dogs.

Let's now turn our attention to our quarry.

2

Whitetail Deer

A deer is a large vegetarian mammal. It eats leaves, plant shoots, nuts, fruit, corn, soybeans, and other plant matter. It lives in mountains, in swamps, and on flat-lands.

There are four species of deer in North America, the whitetail (Odocoileus virginianus), the mule deer (Odocoileus hemionus), elk (Cervus Canadensis) , and moose (Alces alces).

Of these four species of North American deer, moose are the biggest and bull moose can weigh up to 1,300 pounds. Elk are the second largest and bull elk can weigh up to 700 pounds. The biggest whitetail or mule, deer that you will ever see will not likely weigh more than 300 pounds, and will most likely weigh between 100 and 200 pounds.

The arrangement of antlers is another way to differentiate between these four deer species. A moose's antlers will have large palms that extend to the sides and to the back of his head. An elk's antlers will have a main beam that extends backwards, with additional points sticking up from the main beam. Whitetail and mule deer have main beams that curve up, out, and then forward over their heads, with additional points sticking up from the top of the main beams.

Mule deer live in the western part of North America, on plains and around the Rocky Mountains. Whitetail deer live to the East of the Rockies and plains. Whitetails prefer heavy woods, marshes, farmland, and suburban wooded areas. Mule deer live on prairies and fields.

Mule deer get bigger than whitetails. Whitetail deer are more brown, and mule deer are more gray. Mule deer get their name from their very large ears, which apparently resemble the ears of mules. Mule deer will a have dark gray patch between their ears and eyes, that whitetails do not have.

The antlers of mule deer are a bit different than those of whitetail deer too. Both species have a large main beam and grow points up from that beam. Any number of points may grow on whitetail antlers (usually 2 to 12), but mule deer will typically only have 3 points growing up from each main beam. Of these, the first points may, or may not, be there, and they will likely be less than an inch long if they do exist. The second point away from the head will bifurcate. All typical whitetail points will be I-shaped, and the mule deer's bifurcated second points will be Y-shaped.

Whitetails are much more numerous and live near where more people live. So whitetail deer are the most popular North American big game animal.

The other North American large deer sized ungulate (hoofed mammal) is the pronghorn (Antilocapra Americana). Pronghorn are "near-antelope," not deer. Pronghorn have horns and deer have antlers. The difference is that horns start growing when the animal is small and never stop growing. Antlers grow each spring and fall off each winter. Horns also grow on females, whereas antlers usually grow only on the males. Recognize pronghorns by their two horns which each have two points.

Some hunters may refer to deer antlers as "horns", but that is slang, and not actually correct.

There are three main subspecies of whitetail deer: the standard variety, the Florida Key deer, and the Coues.

The standard variety is the biggest of the three; an adult may weigh between 90 to 400 pounds. The Florida Key deer is a small version (up to 75 pounds) of the standard whitetail that lives in the Florida Keys. They are very small and very few in number. The Coues deer is native to the southwestern United States and northern Mexico. Its size maxes out at around 120 pounds. The Coues also lives in different terrain then the other two types. They live in deserts and mountains, whereas the other two varieties live in forests and swamps.

Other than size and location, the only physical difference between the whitetail deer species is that the Coues will often have large white patches of hair where the other types do not. Except for albinos, whitetail deer are brown, or gray, with white hair on their bellies and a few other places. The Coues deer may also have large white patches about itself on its sides, back, neck or head.

Note that albino deer, which have all-white bodies and pink eyes, are often illegal to shoot. Check your local laws.

The whitetail deer is named for the white underside of its tail. The top of the tail is brown, like the back of the deer and white on the bottom. When a whitetail is "spooked" it will run away with its white tail held straight up. Other deer take this as a sign that a deer is running away from potential danger. Usually a deer keeps its tail down so that the brown top will cover the deer's white butt and be more camouflaged.

If you see a deer running away silently, while keeping its tail down, then its probably a buck. When does run away they often want every other deer to know that there is danger here, and so run with their tails up and they make noises. Bucks just want to silently disappear.

When we talk about living whitetail deer we often refer to them by their age class. For example: the buck I shot this year (2013) with a bow was a 4 ½.

Deer are born in the spring, May and June in Wisconsin, later in the south, and are about a half year old during the hunting season. These are known as fawns. There are doe fawns for does, and buck fawns for males. The buck fawns will have two small lumps between their ears where their antlers will be next year.

When a buck's second season comes around he will be 1 ½ years old, the next year 2 ½, the next 3 ½, and so on. I don't know why this is the way we refer to bucks, but I suspect that it is because 2 ½ is easier to say than 30 months and is more accurate than 2 years.

Nowadays when we consider a buck's antlers we think of its age class. A 1 ½ year old whitetail deer might have two points, three, four, and up to eight. (On the opening day of the 2011 archery season I saw a 1 ½ with eleven points. That is very rare.) Whether a 1 ½ has two or eight (or eleven) points doesn't really matter. The scores and the sizes of those deer will be about the same. A 1 ½ is as big as most other 1 ½ year old deer, usually.

There is a bit more size variation in 2 1/2 year old bucks, but a 2 ½ is going to be about the same size as most other 2 ½. The sizes of antlers will vary a bit more as the deer's age increases, but each age will have a standard size range.

A deer's body size and antler size will get bigger each year until it reaches six or seven years old. At this point its body and horns will grow smaller each year. For perspective, I have personally seen less than a handful of deer over 5 years old in my fifteen years of deer hunting.

The size range for each age class is different between where they are located because deer in different climates grow their antlers at different rates.

Here in central Wisconsin a 1 ½ will have from 2 to 8 points. A 2 ½ year old buck here will generally have either eight or ten points and have a gross B&C score from 100 to 120. A 3 ½ will have eight to twelve points and may have a gross B&C score from 120 to 135. And so on. Those are rough estimates, but you should get the idea. And you'll learn how to score your own antlers later, in the appropriate chapter.

Bucks in colder places, such as Northern Wisconsin, or Ontario, are likely to have shorter, heavier antlers. And bucks in the South are likely to have longer, thinner antlers.

You may also guess the age of a buck by looking at the proportions of its body. A 1 ½ will look thin, lean and have a long pointy nose. A 2 ½ will look a bit bigger, more filled out , and appear to have a shorter nose. A 3 ½ will have a short nose and have a square shape to its body. At first you will not be able to tell them apart by their body size, but once you see a few in the woods you will begin to be able to tell the difference.

We might refer to does by their age class, but they are not as easy to tell apart and as far as I'm concerned an antlerless deer is a fawn or a doe. My dad finds the hunters who claim to have shot "really big does" to be amusing. Unless it weighed four hundred pounds, its just a doe.

A doe will usually have two fawns, one buck and one doe, each spring. They will stay with their mother until the following spring when the doe will drive the buck fawn away. During the hunting season you might see one fawn alone, two fawns alone, or a doe with one or two fawns. In all my years of hunting I have never seen a doe with more than two fawns. And fawns who have lost their mothers will be forcefully driven away by adult does.

Covert   08.07.2012 20:08:27

A deer is ready to mate when it is 1 ½. I have seen deer mating two times during my hunting career. And contrary to the idea that it is the biggest bucks that mate the most, one was 1 ½ and the other was 2 ½.

A whitetail deer is considered mature when it reaches 3 ½. Most bucks don't make it to 3 ½. Although their odds are better, most does don't make it that long either. There is also a bit of a trend in hunting magazines and TV shows to call 4 ½ year old bucks fully mature, or similar. This is probably unnecessary. And anyway, if you are of the sort to think that, then I doubt that you need to read a book aimed at the average deer hunter.

Whitetail deer live in forests, wood lots, agricultural fields, marshes swamps, parks, and our yards. They adapt very well to living in the wooded areas in cities. A surprising number of very big bucks have been shot in Milwaukee and Waukesha Counties, WI, which are nearly entirely urbanized. The Minneapolis suburbs, and Duluth also have some exceptional hunting. If you are looking to expand your hunting locations, be sure to check out special hunting laws in metropolitan areas and parks.

In the fall, during hunting season, the deer enter a time of the year known as the "rut." This is when all of the does get bred and the bucks are at their most active for the year. Where I hunt the rut occurs during the first week of November. In the South it takes place during December or January. This will be the peak hunting time for bucks.

Because the rut is the most active time of year for deer it is also the most common time of year to hit a deer with your car. (I don't want to point fingers, but someone I know crashed his dad's truck into an eight point buck each of the last two years a week before the Wisconsin firearms season. But let's not dwell on that.)

Whitetail deer are crepuscular, that is they are most active at dawn and dusk. Big bucks often "go nocturnal" for much of the year, in order to avoid people and other predators. Often it is during the rut when the bucks are chasing does gives you your only chance to shoot the biggest bucks during daylight, hours.

The biggest bucks are often nocturnal by nature and spending too much time in the woods when you shouldn't be there and not concerning yourself with being stealthy while you hunt may cause the bucks to "go nocturnal" too.

A deer likes to be in the woods during the day and in the open at night. Deer trust their noses and ears and being in the woods helps them to identify threats with their noses and ears. Deer also have good night vision and are better able to notice threats in the open at night.

Whitetail deer are crepuscular ungulates that live in North America, east of the Rockies. They are vegetarian and the bucks grow a new set of antlers, not horns, each year.

3

Whitetail Deer Antlers

A deer's antlers are an object of admiration and desire for many.

One common misconception among non-hunters is that a deer will grow one point for each year that it is alive. This is not true. As I described in the previous chapter, a bucks antlers will generally be of an approximate size, and point number, which will be about the same as other bucks of the same age and of the same general location.

The way hunters describe a deer's antlers is either as the deer's age group, 1 ½, 2 ½..., as the antler's width, as its point total, or as its "score."

You can generally tell the age of a buck by the size of its horns, but this is not always accurate. A 1 ½ will have two points to eight points. No matter the number of points a 1 ½ will have antlers that go straight up from the head and not spread away from each other with more than a few inches between them.

It was once often thought that the 1 ½ bucks with only two points (spikes) had inferior genetics to the others. And many hunters shot those small bucks so that they wouldn't breed. Most likely is that this is a buck that was a late fawn, and over time will catch up. A buck's first set of antlers is usually small and they will be bigger next year no matter how big they were the first year. A buck born later in the year (June) might well be smaller than his peers who were born in April or May.

There is a story in "One Man's Whitetail" by Gene Wensel, (which you should read) about a buck that lived on a deer farm. That buck had two points at 1 ½ and, with better food and less stress than it would have in the wild, it eventually grew antlers bigger than the world record. (Deer grown on farms can get to be amazingly big, but they do not meet the requirements in order to become world records.)

If you are going to say that spikes have inferior genetics, then say it because you want an excuse to shoot a buck and not because you believe it to be true. (I'll take all of the excuses that I can get.)

An interesting bit of trivia about deer antlers is that if a deer's back leg gets damaged, the following years' antlers will be odd on the other side. A damaged left back leg will mean an odd antler on the deer's right side every year thereafter. The buck I shot with a gun in 2012 was missing a back leg and had the antler on the other side stuck out sideways.

If a front leg is damaged it is often the antler on that side which will be unusual in the following years.

If you want to describe a buck's antlers by its actual dimensions, then the standard way to do so is by its width and number of points. I may say, "I shot a 14 inch eight." And all hunters will know that the buck I shot has its beams 14 inches apart and has eight points. The first day I ever went deer hunting, my dad shot an 18" ten. Once you see, and measure, enough bucks, then you will know exactly what that means.

The most accurate way to describe a buck's antlers is by its score. In a later chapter I will describe how to score a whitetail buck yourself.

A game animal's score will be its Boone & Crockett score. Boone & Crockett (or B&C, www.boone-crockett.org) is an organization that, among other things, keeps the world record book for North American big game animals. B&C has scored North American big game animals for more than 60 years. They keep records for bears, elk, moose, bison, walrus, etc.

For better or worse, right or wrong, a game animal's score is its B&C score.

One other antler scoring system is the one from the Safari Club International (SCI). While doing research for this book I rediscovered the SCI scoring system, but I am unable to learn about it without paying to join SCI. (Note to SCI: if you want your scoring system to become more widely used, then make the system more freely available.)

If you shoot a buck with a gun or bow, hit it with your car (not recommended), or find it dead, then it may potentially become a B&C world record. There are some requirements including: shooting your animal in "fair chase" and the official scoring must be done after a 60 day drying period.

The drying period occurs because when deer are alive there is some liquid in the antlers, and after the deer die its antlers shrink a little when they dry out. Antlers are scored after a drying period so that all scoring is consistent.

Pope & Young (P&Y, www.pope-young.org) is another organization that, among other things, keeps game animal record scores. P&Y, however, only accepts animals shot with a bow, and there are other requirements. P&Y uses the same scoring system as was invented by B&C.

The B&C scoring system favors symmetry. A deer's antlers are usually symmetrical, but B&C is very picky about both antlers being the exact same size.

In a later chapter I will describe how to score your buck's antlers, and when I do so I will outline some of the basics for B&C and P&Y scoring. For now, understand, that those two organizations are the only ones to be interested in...at least until you well exceed the basics contained in this book, or acquire other hunting interests.

A deer's antlers may be typical, or non-typical. A typical set of antlers, roughly, is a set of antlers with the same number of points on each side, and for whitetails all points stick up from one of the two main beams. Non-typical antlers may have drop tines, stickers, bifurcated tines, etc.

A world record book records all of the bucks ever shot over a stated sizes. In order to be entered into the B&C world record book a typical whitetail must net score at least 170. And a non-typical whitetail must net score at least 195.

The world record typical whitetail was shot by Milo Hansen in Saskatchewan in 1993. Its official B&C net score is 213 5/8.

The world record non-typical whitetail was found dead in Missouri. Its official B&C net score is 333 7/8.

Despite the non-typical having larger antlers, it is the typical record which is meant when someone says "world record." The average deer is "typical" after all.

You can go to deer farms and shoot deer bigger than the world records. They will not be allowed into the world record books, but they can be very big. Expect to pay more than $10,000 to shoot a buck over 200 B&C points.

4
3 Steps to Shooting Deer

If you want to be successful in deer hunting, then I believe that there are only three things that you need to do. Of course there are many things you can do and buy which will help you to be successful, but if you only do these three things well, then I believe that you can still do everything else wrong and still shoot bucks.

Covert   02.10.2012 17:48:09

1. Find a Good Spot

This first thing you need to do is find some land where there are deer. If there are no deer where you are hunting it does not matter how good a hunter you are you cannot shoot what isn't there. An average hunter on a great property is probably going to shoot more deer than a great hunter on an average property. If you don't have a great property, than the single best thing you can do is to get to work to find some better spots.

A good spot can make a hunter more successful than anything else. If you are deer hunting where big bucks live you'll only really need one to wander by in order for you to get lucky.

The skill of a deer hunter may not be accurately judged by the number or size of bucks shot, because a good spot can overcome a lot of a hunters deficiencies. The skill of a hunter might be better judged by the frequency of his shooting the biggest deer in the area. In some places the biggest deer may only be considered medium sized in better spots.

No matter how good the spot you will not always get an opportunity every time, or even see a deer every time that you hunt.

2. Hunt as Much as Possible

Once you've got hunting access on the best property you can get, the next "trick" is to hunt it as much as possible. Even if your location is great, and you are a world-class shooter you can't shoot deer if you are not there to see them.

How many times have you missed a day, or slept in and then had your friends all shoot deer or catch fish while you stayed in? If you are like me, then once was too many. So go more often, and stay out longer than your friends and family and you will not miss out on an opportunity, and you'll probably be more successful than they are.

This point, and having a good spot, are to what I attribute my success. I'll compare my ability to stay on stand with anyone, wind, rain, sleet, snow, sub-zero temperatures... I have sat through it all and I have taken advantage of the opportunities presented to me.

I'm serious about being out a lot. For perspective I hunted 29 out of 30 consecutive days at one point during the 2012 season. As another point of interest I had meant to finish this book by September 2013 and yet I am just finishing it much later because I have been doing nothing but working, hunting, sleeping, and driving between all three (I don't want to know what it is that I have been eating).

I recently read a deer hunting article by, or about, a guy nicknamed: "Ironbutt." He should be my new hero, yours too if you want to shoot big deer.

The more you hunt the more likely you are to have a big buck walk by you.

However, and it's a big "however," If you only have one spot, and by that I mean only one tree, then over-hunting that spot is a real probability. You need to hunt as much as possible in as many places as possible. Ideally, you'll hunt every day of the season but only sit in the same tree for a day or two a month. That's not really possible, or practical for most of us, but that is the way you should be thinking about it.

If you hunt "only" one piece of private property it may be worth your time to spend some time hunting public land too.

Hunt as much as possible, but move around a lot. If the deer learn that you're there, then they won't be.

3. Hit What You Aim At

If you've found your spot and you are there, then the only thing left is to shoot the deer. There is a lot less purpose in hunting if you can't shoot the deer that you see.

A good, sighted in, weapon and practice are the things you need done in order to shoot deer.

The more you practice shooting the better you should get at shooting. Ideally you will be practicing from whatever position, elevation, climate, time of day, whichever clothes, etc. that you will be hunting. And at a deer sized target, from awkward positions, several hours each day, and...

The more the better, so shoot as much and as often as you can.

However, no matter how good you are at hitting a target you will miss deer. The excitement of the hunt, and possibly, your inexperience will mean you don't get every deer you see, but that is part of what adds to the excitement and challenge of deer hunting.

So, that's all you need to do in order to shoot and antlered deer. I believe that you can do everything else wrong and still have a chance to shoot a buck.

5
Where Deer Live

Whitetail deer live throughout much of North America, through Central America, and into Northern South America. Somewhere in the plains states (the Dakotas, Kansas, Nebraska...) Whitetails give way to mule deer. Mule deer live in the plains and mountains, and whitetails live in the eastern forests, fields, and swamps.

Whitetail deer will live anywhere they have the room. They live in and around agricultural fields, in state forests, in swamps, and in large parks. Anywhere they can find enough to eat and some cover, they will live.

Some places are, of course, more favorable than others. And, of course, some places grow bigger deer than other places.

Every state that has whitetails has grown big deer. But the states that are known for producing the biggest bucks are: Illinois, Iowa, Michigan, Missouri, Ohio, parts of Texas, and Wisconsin. You may well shoot big bucks elsewhere, but if you wanted to move to where there are lots of the biggest whitetail bucks, then you best bet will be along the Mississippi River in Illinois, Iowa, parts of Texas, Central Wisconsin, or northern Minnesota.

Because the B&C and P&Y organizations record all the bucks killed over a certain size they have the data to show where lots of the biggest bucks have been killed. Check them out for more data specific to your area. But keep in mind others have done the same thing, and land prices are likely to be higher in the places known for growing big bucks.

Most specifically, you'll find the biggest bucks in the thickest, densest, cover around. If you're unfamiliar with a new property, then find the densest cover and then plan to hunt on the edges of it. You should have a difficult time moving through the best areas. If you enter that cover, then you may drive the deer out of it. Your best spots may well be the biggest trails that come out of those dense areas.

6
Alternatives to Private Land

Now that we know a little about whitetail deer, let's consider where you want to buy your hunting property. Before we do that, though, consider if you really want your own hunting property.

Owning, or renting, your own dedicated hunting property is a great thing to do. You'll have your own deer, sort of. You can improve their habitat. You'll have a good financial investment. You can grow deer food. You can make money having your property logged. You can watch the same deer throughout the year, and from one year to the next. And so on.

Shooting a big buck over a food plot that you've created yourself is a great feeling.

But there are alternatives to owning your own hunting property.

You could hunt public property. If you don't have much money, then it may be your only option. It will not cost you anything, in terms of money. And you will be able to hunt in all sorts of areas. Some great big bucks have been shot on public property. There are large expanses of publicly accessible throughout the Midwest and Canada. Even in highly populated like New England there are all sorts of public hunting properties for you to explore.

If you don't want to hunt public land, and you don't have much money, then you might ask for permission to hunt from landowners.

(You can ask me, but my answer is "No.")

Some things to consider when asking to hunt someone's property: ask permission in late winter or early spring, not right before the season starts. When you ask permission make sure that your truck is clean and your clothes are clean and presentable. Always be polite, and be respectful. Your chances of gaining access for bowhunting only, or late season only are better than obtaining permission for gun season; start with small goals. When you are rejected, always ask the farmer if he knows another landowner that might allow access.

After you get permission, don't ever block a road. Always close gates. And always let the landowner know exactly where and when you be hunting. Offer to give the land owner some meat if you are successful. If you have some money, then you might ask if you could rent, or lease, the hunting rights to a property.

If you are going to get permission to hunt someone else's land, then you'll need to ask every year. Once you have permission to hunt there are things that you should do in order to be allowed to continue to hunt there, close all gates behind you, don't block roads with your car, and expect that, at any time, you will be told not to come back. Even through no fault of your own, you may be asked to leave. You should still be polite and nice and maybe you'll be let back in a year or two. Don't burn any bridges.

A hunting idea that I find very interesting will require money, but gives you lots of freedom. Rather than buy your own property, why not travel to a new game farm or hunting camp each year?

If you only hunt for a week, or two, each year, then traveling to a deer farm is a good idea. There is no need to own, maintain, and pay taxes on a property if you will only use it for a week a year.

One year you may want try a guided hunt Buffalo County, Wisconsin, Pike County, Illinois, or Canada You could try a ranch in Texas the next year, and one in Kentucky the third year. You may find a place that you like and return every year, or you could travel all over to shoot deer.

It wouldn't just be your location that is variable, but the species you target as well. Hunt whitetails in Iowa this year, travel to Colorado to hunt elk next year, shoot a Kudu in Uganda... You could travel the world on different hunting trips rather than be tied to one place.

Another benefit of this plan is that you would be able to skip a year if finances are tight, or get another hunt in if you get a big bonus. Property taxes and mortgages must be paid every year.

When you travel to a deer farm, or ranch, then you may also get opportunities at more and bigger bucks. The owners of farms, and ranches, are professionals at growing lots of big bucks, and then putting their paying customers on the deer. On your own property you'll need to do everything yourself.

There are even places where you can pick out your deer and then you'll hunt that particular buck. One place near where I lives points out that, because of their high fence, you don't need a license; you can use a gun, a bow, or a spear, or whatever. Pick your animal, pay your fee, and then shoot your animal. I have never done it, but for people that have more money than time it may be the best option. For only a few hundred bucks you can shoot a small buck at one of these places and gain experience, which will help you elsewhere.

There is a lot to like about traveling for different hunting situations, and it could be lots of fun. These places should also be able to provide practice for those of you who want a professional around when you shoot your first deer.

7
Public Land

Some of you will not be able to afford to buy land for the purposes of hunting. There are still some options for you.

If you don't have access to any hunting property, then your first job is to find some.

One thing to remember about hunting is that if you do essentially the same thing that everyone else does, you are going to have essentially the same results.

The first thing to do is to ask your friends and family if you can hunt with them. Even if they don't have a hunting property one of them might have a farm, or a very large backyard, or access to some other kind of deer holding land.

Be sure to ask nicely and offer to do yard work or farm work in exchange for hunting rights. You might also offer give some venison to the landowners if your hunt is successful.

Asking farmers, or other large landowners, to hunt their property has a shot at working too. Farmers own land to farm it, and not all of them hunt. Many farmers will lease the hunting rights to their property.

Make sure that you do not park your car on farmers' roads, or in front of their gates. Getting in the way of farmers or leaving their gates open is a good way to annoy someone who's opinion is important to your ability to hunt.

You might not be able to afford a property just for hunting, but when you buy a house you might buy the house that comes with a few acres of land rather than the house in the city. Even ten acres is hunt-able, if not preferable. Properties that small can be improved just like larger properties can be improved.

Once you've asked friends, family, farmers, other large landowners, and maybe you work for a company with a large wooded area around the office, then your last two options are to hunt on a deer ranch when you can afford to, or to hunt public land.

Hunters have had success on public land. Some things to keep in mind are that you'll need a light weight hang on or a climbing treestand, everyone else has just as much right to be there as you do, have a second spot ready if someone gets to your spot before you do, and the places that are easy to get to may have other hunters there already.

If you live in the most of the whitetails range, you should be able to find good hunting if you are willing to put in the effort. One of my friends does well on nice bucks and only hunts the 3 acres on which his grandmother lives I know another hunter that does very well on large bucks and only hunts city and state owned land in a metro area that is accessible to anyone. You need to use your head and explore all possible options.

One trick to hunting public property is to hunt where it is the most difficult to get to. The harder it is to get there the fewer hunters you'll need to compete with.

One of my uncle's friends often hunts an honest 1.7 miles into a National Forest. Last season he shot the seventh buck that he saw. He never saw another hunter. Another family friend does very well hunting way back in the cattails in a large public hunting ground. One of his secrets is that the best hunting is hunting the late bow season after gun hunters have pushed the deer further back into the thick stuff. But bigger land parcels aren't always better, I know of a 40 acre Waterfowl Reproduction Area that very few deer hunters ever set foot on, but those who do have done very well. From the road it looks like 40 acres of marsh grass, but there is a small clump of trees on a back corner that is a major bedding area.

I know of another public hunting area in Wisconsin that used to be open to deer hunting by permit only. Every year the permits sold out. Then state eliminated the permit system on this property and now hardly anyone goes there. There are apparently more deer there now than ever. I guess people just assumed it was better when access was hard to come by.

33

The flood plains of major rivers are often owned by the utility companies and open for public hunting. Many of the large islands on the big rivers are also open to the public. I have a friend that hunts public land along the Wisconsin River that he accesses by boat. He does very well. Another time proven tactic is to take a bow stand on public land the opening day of pheasant season. Why not let all those bird hunters drive some deer to you?

If you are hunting crowded public land, make sure that you have a backup spot. If someone is in your spot before you get there, then you'll need a another location so you don't miss a morning or afternoon hunting because someone crowded your spot.

Some hunters fear being shot by other hunters on public land, but the statistics will show that driving to the public land is more dangerous than getting shot by another hunter. If you are going to get shot while hunting, then it will almost certainly be you that is doing the shooting. Don't let a fear of other hunters deter you from going out. You don't want to hunt where there are lots of other hunters anyway. Hunt where they are not.

Other hunters are a concern on public land, and so are the rules which may be different for each piece of hunting land. Many parks and national/ state forests have laws unique to them.

Many states and provinces will create maps and other things to inform the public where the public land is. The Wisconsin Department of Natural Resources has a thing called: "Public Access Lands Atlas of Wisconsin", which highlights all the public land in Wisconsin.

Another place you can look is to find a "plat book" of the county you want to hunt. You can buy these books from your county courthouse, which are maps of all of the properties and property owners in the state. Get a plat book of the county you want to hunt and then look at your state's hunting laws to see which places are available for hunting, and for their particular laws.

There is also private land that is enrolled in "Managed Forest Land," some of which is open to the public. In Wisconsin, there are 31,500 properties enrolled in MFL programs. Check with the department of natural resources in the state that you live to get a list of those open to the public.

Another option is to check out farms that receive crop damage payments. Many of these must allow some access. Check with the department of natural resources in your state to learn more about these properties.

One of my father's friends who has access to some exceptional private land in central Wisconsin, decided a few years ago to leave that property and start hunting one of the large northern National Forests. The first year he shot 4 bucks including on 150" class buck. (Shooting that many deer is legal in Wisconsin, but during the gun season only, and only when you hunt with others who have not filled their tags.) This past year he shot a 130" class buck. He prefers hunting the less pressured deer of the far north and has been very successful at it.

Find the places that are hardest to get to, or get less hunting pressure, use a climbing treestand, and always be prepared to hunt another spot if somebody else gets there first.

The actual hunting part of hunting public land will be the similar to hunting anywhere else, and will be covered in this book in the appropriate chapters.

8
Choosing a Property for Purchase

Hunting public property may be necessary because you have little money, and traveling to deer ranches each year have their benefits, but if you want to hunt a lot and shoot deer that you "grow" yourself, then the unquestioned best way to do that is to buy your own hunting property and improve it.

Land is also a financial investment that rarely goes out of style.

Once you've decided that you want to buy your own land, and you have the money (it is just like buying a house, but interest rates on loans may be a bit higher), then you need to decide where.

One way to decide where is to look at where lots of the biggest bucks have been shot in the past. There is a map for sale that highlights where all the bucks that are entered in the B&C and P&Y record books have come from. Southeast Texas, Wisconsin, and Illinois along the Mississippi River are the top places.

But none of those places will do you any good if you live in, for example, Pennsylvania. But that's okay because great big bucks have been shot in Pennsylvania and Georgia, and Maryland, and New Hampshire, and Ohio…

If your goal is to hunt a lot, or to shoot a great bug buck (in which case you'll need to hunt a lot), then you should find a hunting property near where you live. Owning a hunting property that is very close to where you live will make it easy for you to hop over and hunt whenever you have some free time during the season. A hunting property that is too close, however, will possibly mean that you want to go over all the time, to cut firewood, or hike, or watch birds, or whatever, and too much people activity on your property will drive deer away.

Having your hunting property less than an hour from where you live is ideal. If it is further away than you'd care to travel regularly to, then you'll want to plan for where you'll sleep if you are going to hunt for a few days in a row.

The biggest problem with hunting close to where you live is the price of the land. If you live in a big city, then you will be competing with all of the other city dwelling hunters who also want land less than an hour from where they live. This competition will drive the price up. The further you get from large cities the cheaper, generally, the land will be.

Quality soil grows quality crops and quality crops grow quality deer. Buying land with good soil should be high on your priority list. But farmers will want farmland with good soil too, and you're unlikely to outbid farmers looking to expand. Finding the un-tillable land in areas surrounded by very expensive farmland will almost certainly produce big deer.

Water is important too. Deer are creatures of drainage systems. A property with a creek or river would often be preferred over one that does not.

You can find out if an area is good by looking for local deer record keeps, like the Wisconsin Buck and Bear club. If your local hunting organization shows that lots of guys are shooting big bucks in your area, then you have a "good area."

But don't overlook a place just because it is not obvious. Owning a small swamp that is surrounded by agricultural fields would mean that you own the best cover in an area surrounded by food, which you'll not need to plant. And that place may just look like a soggy, brushy, useless piece of land.

The land type can be of any sort. Deer live in farm fields, woods, hills, marshes, and peoples' backyards. Any type of land can be good or bad. I would be hesitant to buy a field, however. If all you own is a field, then you won't have any cover which is very important to deer. A property that has lots of big trees can be cut in a year, but a property without trees will need many years to grow trees big enough to put stands in. But you might be able to rent the farming rights to your land with a nearby farmer and you'll get some income.

You do not want to have a property that is mainly plains or prairie grasses. You do not want land that is between highways.

You do not want to be adjacent to city boundaries or major roads. (Cities often do not allow hunting with guns.)

The ideal property will likely include, or be adjacent to a big impenetrable marsh. A big marsh may well be where the biggest bucks in a given area live because it's difficult to get to and will therefore have fewer predators and less human activity. But every place is different, and the thickest tangles of brush are good bedding areas too.

One thing to look for in hunting land is the size of the neighbors' properties. Properties that are deer hunted will usually have the same number of guys hunting them no matter the size. The land owner, his brothers, sons, and nephews will generally all hunt a property weather it is 40 acres or 640 acres. Having a few large landowners as neighbors is preferable to having lots of smaller land owners; more hunters mean more competition.

Access to the land is important to consider. Ideally it will be a little difficult and awkward to get to your hunting property. Land that is easy to get to is more likely to have trespassers and is more likely to have other noises that deer would prefer not to have nearby. Land that is next to houses, while you, the owner, live far away may mean that the neighbors treat the whole area like their own backyard. Land that is right on top of major roads is more likely to lose deer to cars as well.

Walk around the entire border of the property so that you are familiar with all of the edges. You will want to note trespassing, neighbors' development, and where our neighbors put their hunting stands up.

Buying property is expensive. You may want a relative or friend to split the purchase but you should be careful about doing that, because one of you will likely resent the other. One of you may think that you do all the work and the other gets all the rewards. If you are going to split the purchase, then I would recommend splitting the ownership of the land. Instead of you two paying half the mortgage on 40 acres, you should each own your own 20. That way, if there are disagreements, you will own your own half, and the other guy will own his own half.

In any case, make sure that you get your land documents legally in order.

One more thing to consider is the local hunting laws and the local ordinances. If you are located in the wrong county or too near a city you may not be able to shoot guns. I hear that even if you own land in Iowa you may not get a deer tag every year. Some places in New York will even fine you if you shoot a buck that is "too small." Check out what the local laws are before you spend a lot of money on land.

Once you have your hunting property, you will want to improve it.

9
Neighbor Relations

The very first thing you will want to do with your new property is to put "no trespassing" signs up, and maybe a gate, or fence, along a side, or two.

Buy shiny, new, durable, "no trespassing" signs and surround your property with them. Know that the only thing worse than not having the signs is having worn out signs. Surrounding your property with new signs shows that you are at your property often and that you would notice trespassers.

Sometimes properties have old roads, or trails leaning into them. Block off roads that you don't want to use with logs or fences. Some deer may travel down those roads, but you should block the road at your property line so that it is not too easy for someone to trespass.

You do not want to travel all over your property or have roads all over. But you will need, at least, one entrance road. That road should have a gate that looks solid and well maintained. Like new signs, a solid gate shows that you are serious about not wanting trespassers to enter your property. And no gate, or an old worn out one, shows that you probably don't visit often, and probably wouldn't notice trespassers.

If you add a gate over the main entrance, make it a really big one so that you can get big tractors in someday. You may hire loggers or someone to spread lime on your food plots and you won't want to tear down your gate so that they can get in. I have two 12 foot gates, making a 24 foot opening, so that loggers, tractors and anything else that I may want has no trouble entering.

You will also want to get to know your neighbors. Having a good relationship with your neighbors will make owning a hunting property much more enjoyable.

An early conversation with your neighbors should include the following statement from you: "If you hit a deer and it runs onto my land, just go get it."

Your neighbor will most likely respond the same way. Wounded deer running onto neighboring properties has been known to strain relationships. In many states you are legally allowed to trespass in order to collect a dear that you have shot. But it is always better for you to talk to your neighbors before that happens.

Your neighbors are probably unlikely to give you trespassing problems if you have friendly relations with them.

You may want to take note of when your neighbors are around. If you are trailing a deer, or need help dragging one out, then having friends nearby is good. You should be willing to help with their deer too. Compliment their deer and be pleasant. It is much better to have friendly neighbor relations, than otherwise.

You'll have neighbors who have different hunting goals than you do. This may be frustrating when you let bucks go and your neighbor shoots all that he can. There is not much you can do to move his opinion to where yours is. You might explain that you are letting the small bucks go because they won't get big if you shoot them when they are small. But bringing the point up repeatedly may annoy your neighbor to the point that he wants to shoot lots of small bucks just out of spite.

Don't get too frustrated with a neighbor who shoots small bucks. Its his property and he can do what he likes. And the distance between a property that is filled with big bucks and one that lacks deer may not be far.

A few years ago a neighbor shot a buck fawn which ran 150 yards off of his property and fell right underneath my treestand. I reverse trailed the blood trail to find the hunters and found them coming for the deer. They had only seen a handful of deer, of any size, during the few days prior and I had let several medium sized bucks go, not 200 yards from where they were hunting on that very morning. Despite the fact that we share a property line, they who shoot lots of does and small bucks see a few small deer, and I have had opportunities at lots of sizeable bucks.

It may get annoying when your neighbor shoots a buck, but you just have to accept it and congratulate him. And it may even be a good thing. Younger bucks will often appear before big ones, so if your neighbor always shoots the first buck he sees, he'll rarely have a shot at a big one. It's fine with me if all my neighbors want to shoot small bucks; I hunt enough land, and leave enough undisturbed, so that the big bucks feel safe staying on my property and they avoid the properties where all deer get shot. Big bucks prefer to let small bucks and does venture places first, so that he knows if the place is safe without risking himself.

The biggest problem that you are likely to have is your neighbors putting up their treestands right next to your property line. There is not much you can do about this, unless they trespass. You may want to place a "no trespassing" sign in front of their stand, if they get too close. Or you may prefer to put a "Quality Deer Management Association" sign there instead. A sign that says "QDMA is practiced here" is less confrontational than a sign that says "no trespassing" and should have the same effect.

Sometimes you'll need to put your stand near a neighbor's property. It's a good idea to put these stands up so that they clearly face away from the neighbor's property. Sometimes you need to be near the line, but try not to look like you are hunting over their land.

If you are in a position to prosecute a trespasser, then you should go all out. Once the neighbors hear that you are serious about trespassing, they'll want to avoid inviting your wrath.

If you are reasonable with your neighbors, then they will most likely be reasonable as well. Having people nearby who can help move deer, or tow your truck out can be valuable to have. Think of the golden rule and you shouldn't have too many neighbor problems.

10

Property Improvements

Deer need three things: food, water, and cover. To have the best deer property possible you need to maximize the quality and quantity of all three.

After you've put up your "no trespassing" signs you should plan where you want cover and where you want to add food and water. These improvements will need to take place over a series of years because some aspects take time to grow, and you may not be able to afford all of these improvements all at once. So your property improvement plan should cover the next several years. The first part of creating your property plan is to get close up aerial photos or even draw a map of what you have and where you plan to make your improvements.

Where you want to improve your property will depend largely on what your individual property looks like. Anyplace on your property might be changed into cover, food, or water, but some places will cost a lot less in order to transform them. Moving trees and dirt around is not cheap.

Many successful hunters want their thickest bedding areas in the center of their property, then surround that with fruit and nut trees, and have their food plots around the outside. This arrangement, if you have enough land, will mean that the deer do not need to leave your property and are unlikely to wander into your neighbors'.

Once you've planned where you want things, you'll want to work first on whichever takes the longest to get into shape, or work first on which ever can be done in the season that you are currently in. Tree planting is more difficult in the winter, etc.

Clearing an area for food plots may require removing some trees or stumps. Trees can be felled quickly, but stumps are best removed by someone with a bulldozer several years after the tree was cut. Without a lot of digging, or explosives, a fresh stump will remain firmly attached by its extensive root system. A few years after the tree has been cut the smaller roots will rot and the whole stump can be moved out of the way with a bulldozer. You could use a stump grinder to take the height of the stump down to the ground but the stump will remain a constant irritant whenever you do anything like till that ground. It is best to go around it until you can have it bulldozed. It's a good idea to have all of your stumps removed in one bulldozing session; having the excavator come to your property multiple times will be more expensive than having him come over only once.

Growing food will not be particularly effective in your first season either. It will often take a few years to improve your soil to its peak, and it will take several years for fruit and nut trees to begin bearing fruit. If you want fruit trees, then you had better plant them early in your property improvement.

Creating your water source(s) will not take as long. A professional excavator can create one in a few days or weeks, so long as you can afford to pay for it.

Cover is where the deer will live. It is where they go to sleep and where they go to get away from danger. If you don't have cover, then the deer will spend most of their time on someone else's property. Your property may already have lots of cover and you may not need to add any.

Are there large areas on your property where you have great difficulty walking through? Can you see through those places?

You want a large percentage of your property to be nearly impenetrable to yourself and your eyes. If it isn't food or water, then it might as well be cover. The thickest, most impenetrable, out of the way places would be my bet for where the biggest bucks around live.

How you create, or improve, your property's cover will depend on what you have already, and what your property is like. A wide open space will have no cover; you'll need to plant brushy plants and/ or trees. Here in central Wisconsin white pines grow at around one foot each year starting the year after they are planted. Several rows of coniferous trees are good cover from when they reach a few feet high until they grow too tall to have any low branches.

Fast growing coniferous trees are good, but plant any bushy plant that you know grows fast, if you're converting a field. But watch for plants that are hard to be rid of. You may want to kill off lots of them later, so don't plant things like sumac or buckthorn.

A property that has lots of mature trees does not have any cover. It may seem wrong to cut down most of those mature trees but doing so will provide more benefits than having those trees remain standing. Mature trees may provide some food in the form of nuts, but nothing else. When those trees are cut new plant growth is encouraged, because the sun is able to reach more small plants. New plant growth provides cover in the form of brush and food in the form of browse. "Browse," or fresh plant growth, is a large part of a deer's diet.

A deer can reach about as far off the ground as you can, anything above that is useless to deer.

If its not food or cover, then fix it. Although you will have need for trees for treestands and trees behind your stands so that you are not silhouetted against the sky.

When you hire loggers to cut down your trees they will pay you for the wood. The amount of money that you get will depend on the quality of your wood and how much you want to cut. You'll probably get several thousands of dollars for your wood, even if its of low quality and only good for pulp. If you don't get several thousand dollars for the trees you had cut, then you either have a small property, or you did not cut enough.

You may want to plan your property so that you cut different sections every ten years. The first year or two after you cut will leave you without trees or much cover. After a few years the new growth will reach a larger size and become great deer cover. But after many years the brush will become another mature forest with limited cover and limited food.

Be sure to clearly mark a few trees for the loggers. You'll want to leave some trees for future tree stands. A tree will take 20-30 years before it is big enough for a stand, and you won't want to wait that long.

Fruit and nut trees are a good way to add some food, but deer will get most of their food from natural browse, which you created by clear cutting. It takes several years for trees to grow big and produce their mast (fruit, nuts, etc). The longer that you wait to plant, the longer it will be before you see any results from them.

Apple, crab apple, pear, and chestnut trees will all provide food for deer. You'll need to fence these trees in, or deer, and other animals, will eat the fresh tree growth and the tree will not get bigger. Wrapping the bottom of the trees may be necessary to

DLCcovert.com   3.10.2008 23:40:06

prevent rabbits from chewing off all of the lower bark too.

You need to plant more than one type of apple tree in order for them to pollinate. It is also recommended to plant a variety of apple, crab apple, and pear trees in your apple orchard in order for them to be properly pollinated. It is good to check when each species ripens. Ideally, some of your apple trees will drop apples in August, some in September, and some in October (or similar, depending on where you are). Having your trees ripen at different times of the year will mean that deer will return to that area for the ripening of each of the apples, rather than only visiting the trees for only one time period.

Growing fields of deer food is another type of food source that you can create. Fields of deer food are known as "food plots." Food plots are just fields, or small areas, of clover, or soybeans, or turnips, or whatever.

Baiting is a third way to add food to your property. Baiting often has all sorts of laws and restrictions associated with it. Check your local laws.

Deer bait might be: corn, soybeans, sugar beets, carrots, apples, or you might go to a farm supply store and buy horse feed, or horse treats. The deer in your area may prefer one kind, or another. And some deer may take some time before learning that new, for them, things are good to eat.

Incidentally, the best baiting technique is to hunt under oak trees or chestnut trees. I once read a magazine article that included a line like: "a deer will walk right over your pile of corn to get at some fallen acorns." The buck I shot while in the middle of writing this had a stomach that, as far as I could tell, was 100% full of acorns.

There are also salt licks, mineral licks, and flavored sugar goo. There is merit to the argument that deer need minerals to grow and you should therefore add mineral licks. You may, or may not, notice a difference if you do add mineral licks. Minerals will have the most impact on antler size when they are eaten by the deer during the season of antler growth. Put minerals out, if you are legally able to do so, during the spring and summer.

Feeders are often used for bait. One reason is to keep the food off of the ground. When food is spread on the ground it will eventually become mixed in with their excrement. That is unhealthy.

I have not had much experience with deer feeders, but they are big business in some parts of the country. My personal preference would be towards feeders that are gravity operated. Electronically operated feeders are more expensive and more likely to break. But timed electronic feeders do have the ability to train deer to come for the food at a regular time.

Baiting is frowned upon by many people. These people may not like adding artificial food sources, or they may not like the convergence of many deer to one place, which they claim results in faster spreading of diseases.

Baiting is also expensive and labor intensive. A food plot or three will provide food without you once they are planted, but bait will need to be physically carried out each time that you want it out.

When celebrity hunters get busted for breaking a law, it is often because they were breaking baiting laws.

Water is another essential for deer survival. Deer get water from all sorts of places. They get it from streams, lakes, and rivers. They also get it from puddles, leaves, and anywhere else that holds water.

If I hunted somewhere where it is hot, then water would be my first land improvement priority. All deer need water, but that is especially true where it is hot.

The thing to do to add water is to hire a local excavator to create a pond. You may need to add a pump, or you may not. Ground tarps and other things may also be necessary to keep the water in. Adding a pond can improve your hunting a lot but it will cost several thousand dollars. Hire your excavator and then do what he says. He's the expert and he knows more than you or me.

Having a long term property plan is good. It is also good to think about where you want your ponds and food plots when you can afford to pay for them.

After clear cutting, and planting more trees, you should think about where your property, and the surrounding area, is weakest in terms of food, water, and cover. Improve whichever is weakest, and then move to the next.

There are all sorts of other exceptionally interesting ways to improve your deer hunting. About a year ago I attended one of Tony LaPratt's Ultimate Land Management boot camps. My dad mostly dragged me there, but I came away hugely impressed. Attending his boot camp will open your mind to a whole new way of looking at deer hunting. He knows how to do things that you would not believe if I listed them here.

I highly recommend Tony's Ultimate Land Management (tonysulm.com) for advanced land management.

11

Food Plots

Food plots are a big trend in deer hunting these days. A food plot is basically a small field. A food plot can be big or small, and you can do it yourself or hire someone to do it for you.

A company that will create your food plots for you is likely to be a guy with an ATV and a small advertisement. He'll be worth finding if you want food plots but do not want to create them yourself.

One other idea is to see if a local farmer will plant part of your property for you. You might pay him to plant yours, pay him to leave a few rows of corn up into the fall on his property, or you may just let him plant his crops on your property and allow him to sell the crops he plants on your property. A farmer won't want to bother with your property if there are not at least a few acres ready to be planted though. And the harvest season ends prior to most of the hunting season, so you will not have the agricultural crops up during the deer season; unless you've just paid him to plant on yours and he does not harvest it. But even early harvested food is still not a bad idea because all that food will keep the deer in your area throughout much of the year.

Each property is different and each property's food plots will be completed in a different sort of way.

The way everyone talks about food plots is that you want a large 'destination plot' and several small 'hunting plots.' The idea is that the destination plot is a field full of corn or soybeans and the smaller plots will have things like clover, chicory, and turnips.

Deer prefer to stay in the thick cover during the day. There they can use their ears and noses to detect threats. At dawn and dusk the deer don't mind being out in the open, where their eyes are suited for low light.

The plan is that the deer will spend the days in the cover, move to the smaller food plots just before heading out to the bigger plot after dark. They'll spend the night in the large fields and then go through the smaller plots after dawn and then head back to cover during the middle of the day.

Many of the biggest bucks will "go nocturnal." Bucks don't get big by living where there is danger. That means that they will prefer to be active only at night. This is a problem because we are unable, and not allowed by law, to hunt during the night. When the deer are mating, "the rut," the bucks will be active whenever the does are. When the bucks are looking for does they will check all of the little food plots before going to the big one. With more little plots he'll need to start earlier to check them all before it gets dark, when he'll be in the big plot.

It may or may not actually work like that, but more plots are good because it means more food, and because a doe will often take over a plot, and kick all other deer out; does can be mean to other deer. They prefer to be alone with their fawns and will drive other deer away. The more plots that you have the more does that can occupy one for themselves. And the bucks will need to move around more during the rut in order to check on each of those does.

Those bucks will start looking through those plots after leaving the cover they spend their days in. You do not want that cover near your property lines because that makes it easy for your neighbors to wander through your cover and drive the deer away. If you can, leaving the middle of your property as cover is best; with your food and hunting around the thick central cover.

Those are the theories with which you will want to lay out your property. Cover, then a bunch of small food plots, and then the big food plot would be the ideal layout.

In practice you will put your big plot wherever you have a large clearing, or a space that can become a large clearing. Your big plot will have the goal of growing as much food tonnage as possible. It does not matter what shape the plot will be. Although the deer would prefer irregular shapes, rectangles are easier to plant. The size of your big plot depends largely on the tools that you have available. Bigger is better, to a point. Your budget may well be the determining factor in regards to your food plot size.

Some things to consider before placing your big food plot will include the ease of access, soil test results, what the plants growing there already look like, and the location relative to the rest of your property.

It does you no good to have a great spot for a food plot if you cannot get the tractor or ATVs to where the location is. The cost of building the road to reach that place must also be considered. If your soil test says that you soil is very poor then it will cost a lot to improve it and you should look for another spot.

Deer would like it if you put you big food plot next to lots of cover, so long as you do not have too much activity there to disturb them. Take note of the land around your property too. It does not help you any to have you food plot located where deer that find cover on other properties only visit your property for food. If that is the case then it is the property owner who has the cover and the area between the cover and the food, who will have the best hunting opportunities.

The dominate wind direction during the hunting season should also factor into you planning. You don't want your treestands upwind of the cover or the food plots. The dominate wind direction here in Wisconsin during the hunting season is from the Northwest. This means that my treestands should not be located on the Northwest end of the property, that corner is better suited as cover.

The smaller food plots can be located anywhere you have some space. The access road to the big food plot can be planted in clover; places where the road can be widened are good place for food plots too. Otherwise, wherever you have any sort of room big enough four your tractor, or ATV, to maneuver around in can be a fine place for a small food plot.

With the smaller hunting plots, irregular shapes are the way to go. Deer don't like being too far from cover. Smaller food plots that are shaped like an S, L, or 8 mean that deer will always be a jump or two from cover.

The ideal shape of a hunting plot, I'm told, is the shape of a bird's foot. This shape is a few lines connecting at a common point. With this arrangement you will sit in the intersection, have shooting lanes, and the deer will be happy to never be further than one jump from cover.

The last thing to consider before creating a food plot is the equipment that you will be using. You could, create your food plots with hand tools and up to tractors. Building food plots with tools smaller than ATVs or lawn tractors mean that you will do an awful lot of work and only get small amount of results. That's what the difference in equipment means: the bigger the equipment, the faster and bigger the plots that you can create are.

My dad and I spent too much time trying to use things like hand sprayers and walk behind tillers to create food plots, but that was mostly a waste of time to spend hours and get tiny food plots. Unless its your only option due to budget or access restraints, using tools less than an ATV are mostly a waste of time. Although any little bit can help.

12

Food Plot Equipment

In order to create a food plot there are some pieces of equipment that you will need, and some that would be helpful.

You'll need a chainsaw to clear brush and trees, and a bulldozer to remove stumps to get started.

An ATV or small tractor will pull many of the farming tools that you will use. An ATV with a solid rear axle will be poor for trail riding, but will be best if you plan to pull implements with it (and you do). Many say Honda Foremans, with solid rear axles, are the best; I do not know enough about them to give you a recommendation.

Spraying herbicide on the plants that are in the way of your food plot, or on the weeds that pop up will require a herbicide sprayer. Herbicide sprayers come in various sizes. Hand held bottles that you pump and then spray with a wand are very small and awkward to carry around in the woods. The smallest sprayer that you'll want to get is a backpack sprayer. If you have an ATV, then you'll want an ATV sprayer. If you have a tractor, then you'll want a sprayer trailer.

After the weeds have been sprayed, you'll need a means of tilling the soil. A walk behind roto-tiller may be ideal for planting a small garden with a handful of tomato plants, but they are nearly useless if you want to plant an area larger than the area covered by your car (and you do).

The very first time that you till a space you will want to rent a tractor or an ATV with something like a four or six foot roto-tiller. The tractor's tiller will likely be attached with a PTO and a three point system, and an ATV will require a tiller trailer with its own motor. Roto tillers break the ground up best and will save you huge amounts of time and effort when opening the ground for the first time.

A disc may be used to till the soil after the tiller has broken it up. And once the tiller has gotten the soil started a disk may be all that is necessary.

In order to spread fertilizer and lime you'll need a spreader that goes over the shoulder, one that you walk behind and push, or one that you pull with your ATV or tractor. The ones that you walk behind are immensely tiring to use on tilled fields, so go with the over the shoulder bag or ATV/ tractor spreader.

A broadcast seed spreader is one that you hold in one hand and crank with the other, the same spreader you used to fertilize, or one that you pull behind an ATV or tractor. A seed drill is the best way to plant seeds. These can be pulled by an ATV or a tractor. They are also likely to be very expensive. If you do not use some sort of seed drill or broadcast spreader, you will waste an awful lot of seed (just like all other novice part-time farmers).

A drag harrow can be used to scratch up soil for seeds that do not need to be planted deeply or to loosely cover seeds spread over disced or tilled soil. A drag will cost a couple of hundred dollars and can be pulled by an ATV, tractor, and perhaps your lawn tractor.

A cultipacker is used like a lawn roller, to pack the seeds into the soil. Seeds left on top of the soil may get pounded in by rain or eaten by birds. Incidentally, I don't like turkeys.

You will use either a drag or cultipacker to cover the seeds once they've been spread. A cultipacker will do a better job but you'll likely need a tractor to pull it and/ or they can be very difficult to find.

A mower is used to trim clover to promote the fresh growth preferred by deer. Your home's lawnmower can do your food plot mowing, but it cuts too short and will really beat your mower up. Ideally you'll have a tow-able mower to pull behind your ATV/ tractor. You don't want to cut more than one third off the height of a plant.

If you have an ATV or tractor you might replace many of the above mentioned tools with an all in one tool like the

Plotmaster. I don't care for all in one items myself. They seem too complicated, do everything poorly, do nothing excellently, and if it breaks you are out all of your tools.

Planting (not counting spreading lime, fertilizer, mowing, etc.) your food plots can be done in two days a year...theoretically. Once in the spring and once in early fall. Two days a year may not be enough to justify the purchase of an ATV or small tractor. You may want to rent one for those two days a year and get everything done on those two days. That's the plan anyways. You won't always get done what you want done in the time frame you have in mind.

My dad and I started with little in terms of food plot tools, and have increased the size, number of tools, and number of hours spent on food plot creation. With that experience I can tell you that walk behind tillers, and the sprayers you carry in one hand and spray with the other are all too small. Don't bother with those, you will be much happier getting the next size bigger or by hiring someone to get your plots done. Learn from our labor and don't bother with food plot tools smaller than ATV sizes.

Ideally, you'll have an ATV, an ATV spreader, an ATV sprayer, a tow-able mower, a tow-able rototiller, a cultipacker, and a hand crank seed spreader, plus a chainsaw.

Even better would be to have a tractor and all the above.

Even if you rent something to do the actual tilling you'll want to own, at least: a backpack sprayer, an over the shoulder spreader, and a hand crank seed spreader.

And so my advice for you beginning food plot creators is to hire a guy to start yours for you. He can get them started while you acquire the tools and knowledge needed to take them over yourself. Getting them started is the hardest part, you may as well have someone else do that for you. Once the ground is flat and level everything will get lots easier.

13

Creating Food Plots

This chapter is an overview of how to create food plots for deer. For more information, you will want to read a food plot specific book, such as: Ultimate Deer Food Plots by Ed Spinazzola.

The steps to create a food plot are: select a location, get a soil test, clear the brush and stumps, add the minerals suggested by the soil test, till, add fertilizer, and then plant the seeds.

The location for your big plot will be wherever you have the room. But the soil test may show that the dirt where you plan to plant will need too many minerals and too much fertilizer to be a good place for a food plot.

A thorough soil test will tell you what type of lime to get and what type of fertilizer you need to add. The difference between getting the soil to its peak and not bothering with a soil test is the difference between growing plants that do little more than sprout and growing plants that reach their potential.

You can grow some plants with poor soil, but your results will be a fraction of what they would be if you improve the soil correctly.

To do a soil test, you will put a small spade's worth of dirt into a plastic bag and then mail it to whoever does your testing, with the appropriate fee, and information about what you intend to grow. And then you will await the results.

Your local university with an agriculture department may do soil tests or you might follow the instructions at BioLogic's website.

Once you receive the results of your soil test you will need to look for whatever the soil test says that you should add to your soil. This will include lime, to correct the soil's pH, and other minerals. If you live East of the Mississippi River, put some lime out now, your soil pH is almost certainly too low, and lime takes a while to affect the soil acidity. And now put some more out, however much you did the first time was not enough. The food plot being tilled by my dad a few pictures ago required twelve tons of lime per acre. You can hire your local farmer's ag supply guy to bring and spread lime for you. Or for small plots, you can pay a lot more, per pound, and get fifty pound bags of lime which you'll spread with one of the above mentioned spreaders.

Try again; still not enough lime out.

Creating a seed bed consists of clearing the brush, spraying with herbicide all the weeds, and then opening the soil with a rototiller, disc, or drag.

After selecting your spots you'll need to clear the brush and the stumps, if you can. You can go around most stumps and trees, food plots are better as irregular shapes anyway, but hiring someone with a bulldozer to remove a few select stumps will greatly increase the size of many of your food plots and greatly increase the ease with which you work on the plots.

After picking your spots and clearing your brush you'll need to create the seed bed

By spraying weeds, I mean once you have your spot selected you need to kill the existing plants to make room for yours. You'll need something like Round-Up, which is 41% glyphosate. Spray this with a backpack sprayer, ATV sprayer, or tractor sprayer. It will take something like ten days to kill everything that is there already. You need to finish spraying at least an hour before it rains. And this will kill existing plants. After a week you'll want to spray again to kill the new sprouts. Twice should be enough.

After the weeds are mostly dead and brown, you'll want to till. If you wait too long, the weeds will pop back up and you'll need to start over. A small garden tiller is too pitifully small, will require lots of work and give you too small of a plot. Hire a guy, rent an ATV or tractor, or buy one.

One non-obvious thing when tilling is to not till too deep. A seed has enough built in energy to grow a plant a few inches. If you plant too deeply, the plant won't make it too the surface. The correct depth is about the diameter of the seed. You should have the diameter of the seed worth of soil over the seeds when you are done tilling.

Once the seed bed is prepared, you'll need to spread your seeds with a spreader. Spreading without a seed spreader is just wasting seeds. Apparently, everyone new to planting, me included, puts way too many seeds out when we first start planting. Spread seeds at the rate recommended on their package. Too many seeds mean that too many plants will be trying to get the same few soil nutrients from a given area. (My guess is that most of you who read this will still spread your seeds way too thickly and waste a lot of seed.) Set your spreader at the smallest opening setting that allows your seeds out and walk fast with the hand crank spreader.

The usual food plot suspects, for your big (destination) food plot, are: corn, soybeans, peas, buckwheat, and wheat. For your hunting plots you may want to grow: clover, oats, chicory, turnips, kale, radishes, and buckwheat. There are several varieties of each of these plants and each have their own advantages and disadvantages. A variety is best, and ideally, you'll have some plants that deer like to eat during each month of the year. You want the different plant to ripe all throughout the year, so that the deer have no need to leave your property for food.

Corn is a great food for deer, but consider if you have tools big enough to clear the corn stalks out next spring before you plant. Soybeans, peas and oats are easier to clear out next year.

The base of your small hunting plots will be a variety (red, white, kura, etc.) of clover. One thing a lot of guys like is to plant clover in the spring, then when ready for the fall planting, they till stripes through the clover so they have alternating plants.

Clover is a perennial. That means that it will come up for years after its planted. Don't expect much the first year you plant anything, but the second year and later clover will grow well and doesn't need maintenance aside from mowing two or three times per deer. Deer like the fresh growth that comes from mowing. And mowing reduces weeds.

If you do get a lot of weeds in clover, first mow, then wait a few weeks to see if that removed most of them. Your next option is a grass-selective herbicide. Grass-selective herbicides should kill grasses and nothing else. If you don't want to find any of that you can use half the ratio of 41% glyposate to water ratio that you use when you spray to clear fields of weeds. Even a full dose of glyposate won't kill clover if it gets enough rain. The clover may turn yellow for a while, but so long as it gets rain, it will bounce back weed free and as good as ever.

Clover is great. Plant it, fertilize it every year and mow two or three times per year and it will pop up in the spring and attract deer throughout the fall. But because it is a perennial you are not maximizing your food plots by only growing clover.

Annuals are plants that grow one year and then die off. That means yearly plantings for you, but every ounce of energy that plant has will be used in order to grow the year its planted. It can't wait until next year. Brassicas like chicory and turnips are annuals that will add variety to your food plots.

Where you are located will greatly determine what plants grow, or grow well. Purple top turnips grow exceptionally well for me, but they may not grow at all where you plan to plant them. And some guys claim that their deer prefer radishes to turnips anyway.

You can mix all of these plants together when you plant, but clover needs to be mowed and mowing brassicas like turnips will prevent them from getting big. Plan accordingly.

You may get name brand, BioLogic, Tecomate, Antler King, etc, seeds at your sporting goods store, or you can get cheaper generic seeds from a feed mill.

If you go to your local feed mill, ask the guy there what sort of plants grow best in your area. If you get name brand seed mixes, look out for rye or ryegrass. Deer will eat it when its short but it will grow tall, shade your other plants and overwhelm your food plots with a plant that has limited food value and is difficult to remove from your plots.

After the seeds are spread they need to be covered, to be in full contact with the ground, and to make it harder for birds to eat them. A cultipacker is best, a drag is okay, and a rototiller set at a depth of a half inch is also okay.

You do not want the seeds too deep. The seeds should be in the soil about as deep as the seed's diameter.

Ideally, a heavy rain will start as soon as you finish covering your seeds. Plant just before it rains if you can, even if that means planting a week, or two, too early or too late. Lots of rain makes up for lots of other mistakes.

Some of these plants need to be mowed. Deer prefer fresh growth, and mowing encourages fresh growth. The mowing height will be a bit higher than your home's lawnmower will cut. You shouldn't cut more than a third off the height of plants, but cut more if your only alternative is to not mow. If your yard's lawnmower is the only mower that you have, then set it at its highest setting. You will want to mow about once a month until about a month before the end of the growing season.

Many of you will read the previous chapter and then ignore the mowing advice contained therein. This will be a mistake, particularly with clover. Clover must be mowed, or grasses will take over.

Many of you will look at your beautiful clover plots and not like the idea of mowing it. Then you may return in two weeks to find minimal clover, lots of grass, and the few places you did mow are the places that look fantastic now.

Mow your clover, but not within thirty days of the first frost.

You will, obviously, not mow anything if you have no rain and no plant growth.

Planting the plants that need to be mowed on your roads and trails is a good idea, because those areas will be cleared anyway and the more food that you have the better.

Plan your planting around how maneuverable your planting tools are, by what needs to be mowed, and what needs to be rotated each year. (Look up "crop rotation" if you don't know anything about it. And don't plant turnips in the same place every year.) If you only have a big tractor, don't expect to be able to make tight turns in a small food plot, for example.

Fertilizer is expensive, but it will greatly increase the amount of food that you grow. Bags off fertilizer will have three numbers on it, such as "10-10-10". The ratio of those numbers is what is important, not the specific numbers. 10-10-10 is ten percent nitrogen, ten percent, phosphorus, ten percent potassium, and seventy percent inert matter. The specific ratio you look for will be recommended in your soil test results.

Many cities ban fertilizer with nitrogen, because all governments are good at screwing with things. Plants don't grow without nitrogen, so go out into the country where there are likely fewer fertilizer regulations and buy it there. (Check your local laws.)

Fertilize after each of your spring/ fall plantings and again in the summer.

In order to limit the weeds in your food plots you may need to spray a "grass selective herbicide." If you do not have a grass selective herbicide, then spraying your clover plots with your normal Round-Up (the name brand grass selective herbicide) equivalent will kill the weeds, and the clover will recover, provided you get some rain. This spraying may consist of half the usual herbicide to water mixture.

You'll want to repeat all the above steps every year, excepting tree and stump removal if they're gone already. After a few years you can skip soil tests every other, or two out of three, years.

Don't worry about scaring the deer while you're creating food plots. So long as you make some noise and don't chase after them, they'll move around you but will be unconcerned about a danger they can hear from a long ways away.

At this point I'd like to tell a short story I read in Gene Wensel's "One Man's Whitetail," A farmer wrote to a deer expert saying that he had deer in his field every night. In the evenings the deer would see him walk from his barn to his house as he ended his day. On some nights they'd look at him and not move, and on others they'd see him and run away. It turns out that the nights when the deer ran away were the nights when he was upwind of the deer. When they could smell him the deer knew that it was just the farmer heading in for the night. When they could not smell him they ran away because they could not be sure it was him.

Making noise through the woods won't scare deer. They'll just move away from the noise. "Something that loud is easily avoided," they'll think. But when you sneak through, if they detect you they'll be nervous about the noises coming from a source they can't always locate.

When you do all of this depends on lots of things. You can look at the seed packages to tell you when to plant, you can check online for dates in your area for specific plants, and you'll come out ahead if you clear all your areas as soon as the snow is gone in the spring and you are set to go in April or whenever your first planting is.

You'll likely have to plant in the spring and again about a month before the season starts. Many hunters only plant in the fall and that can work out, but that means that you'll not have as much food when the fawns are first growing, and you'll be leaving your plots to get a summer's worth of weeds before you plant things yourself.

14

Trail Cameras

Trail cameras are a great way to get an idea of the animals that live on your property. They are also a great excuse to walk all over your property, which will cause the deer to leave.

Personally I think that trail cameras are overused, but they do have their uses.

DLCcovert.com   10-30-2011 19:09:06

If your goal is to shoot the very biggest buck that exists on your property, then having trail cameras out is a way to identify that particular buck and to identify when and where he, specifically, will be at a given time.

A while ago I read a magazine article that described a guy who would put five pounds of corn out each morning at 6:30 and then got a trail camera picture of a big buck at 7. On the day he hunted he had a friend go out with him to spread the corn and then his friend left to make the deer think that the corn provider left. The hunter then shot the buck right at 7. So cameras can be used to great effect, sometimes.

Bucks, and particularly big bucks, are not often this predictable. Bucks don't get big by being stupid.

You are very likely to get exactly one picture of the biggest buck that you get a picture of. They any learn to avoid cameras, or just are very unpredictable. The two biggest bucks shot where I hunt did not appear in one picture, despite multiple cameras being out for six months prior to their shooting. And the biggest bucks I have on camera appeared on camera only once and never in person. Although, that may be because I have a lot yet to learn about going unnoticed by deer.

Identifying the biggest buck around, estimating the number of bucks around, looking at pictures of deer, and having photographic evidence of big bucks that you can show to prospective buyers of your property, should you want to sell it, are the reasons to have trail cameras out.

Seeing picture of bucks is nice but I would not feel bad if none were used where I hunt. I know that the property has lots of deer and big bucks on it already. If I hunt long enough, then I'll get an opportunity to shoot one, or three.

Setting cameras up, exchanging memory cards, and batteries all require you to wander around your hunting property bringing your smells and noise with you. The more you walk around the less the deer will want to be there. At one place my dad and I had a camera we had pictures of a dozen different bucks one week, a half dozen the next, and only around three the next. I took it as an argument that swapping memory cards every week was driving the deer away.

I don't care for trail cameras, but if you want to use one here are some suggestions.

Old film cameras are worthless. You'll only get 24 pictures, which isn't many, you'll need to check it every few days, and developing the film may bankrupt you.

Cameras that have bright flashes may scare deer, go for the black flash cameras instead.

Checking on your camera once per week is too often, and you activity will scare deer. Modern cameras have batteries that will last for months, but checking it twice a season will be of minimal help in directing your hunting activates during the season. And if the camera goes wrong a day after you leave it, then you'll have spent a month collecting zero pictures.

Use the same sight, sound, smell procedures that you use when you are hunting to set up and check cameras. You need to minimize your presence.

A camera at your chest height will be at the right height to capture as much in front of the camera as possible. You'll also be able to get pictures of curious doe noses investigating the camera. This height will also be ideal for getting a deer to notice the camera.

I'm told that putting the cameras up high will make them less visible to deer, because deer don't often look up. But if your camera flashes, or makes a noise, then you may train the deer to look up. And that's not good because a sizeable part of your camouflage is being above the deer's line of sight. Have I mentioned that I don't care for cameras?

I've used cameras from several companies. I've used them enough to know that I am not going to recommend any of them or point you away from any of them. The biggest differences between cameras, of which I can tell, is the quality of the low light pictures and the ease of use. (They can all be a terrible pain to use.)

A new hunter, or new property owner, can derive some advantages to getting an idea of what sort of deer you have on your property. This will be especially useful when we determine what size deer you should shoot in a later chapter. But once you have an idea of the size and number of deer on your property, then I recommend forgetting about them, or not replacing them when they break, which they will.

A neighbor did get a picture of my biggest buck to date about a month before I shot him.

Many people want to share pictures of bucks with everyone. Some show pictures of dead bucks. And some, show pictures of bucks from trail cameras. I've noticed that those two groups of people never mix; either they shoot deer or they are happy to show everyone pictures of deer they will never shoot.

You know what's better than stupid cameras? Going out and watching the deer for yourself.

15

Hunting Methods

Now that you've found your deer hunting property, perhaps improved it, and maybe identified a particular buck, then it is time to plan your actual hunt.

There are a few methods used to hunt deer.

Hunting deer with dogs was not uncommon at one time. These days it is often illegal to hunt deer with the aid of dogs. I have not hunted deer with dogs, and don't know how it is done. My understanding is that it is not much practiced these days.

If you want your dog to be involved in your deer hunting, then training him to collect shed antlers is a fine way to do so. Search the internet for dog trainers to help you with that. Or visit a hunting exposition. There will likely be dog trainers exhibiting there, and they should be able to help you out. But keep in mind that a dog chasing deer is a fine way to drive deer away from your property.

One of the reasons that hunting with dogs is not common is the same reason tracking deer is uncommon in much of the country. The owner of many hundreds, or thousands, of acres may have enough land to track deer, but the average hunter will not have the amount of land necessary to do so. There is not much point in tracking deer across your 40 acres if you can only do so for a few hundred yards before the deer moves onto your neighbor's property.

It is my understanding that the deer hunters in Northern New England are the hunters who hunt by tracking. There is lots of public hunting land in Maine, New Hampshire, and Vermont. The public hunting in those states is large enough for you to follow a deer's tracks for miles without trespassing.

The family that is always mentioned as the best deer hunters is the Benoits. There are several books written to describe how they hunt deer by tracking them and that is where you'll want to turn your attention if tracking deer is what you want to do.

I wouldn't recommend tracking deer in the large uninhabited lands if you are not at least very familiar with the area in particular. By wandering for miles, you'll need to keep a close eye on where you are, and pay attention to the weather. Deer season runs through the fall and winter. Your survival skills will need to be good if order for you to track deer safely.

Many parts of the country still hunt deer by doing deer drives. Deer drives require lots of hunters, and lots of land to do well. With our culture of not being as friendly with our neighbors as we once were, and the preference to own our own land and not lets friends walk all over it, many places have seen a large decline in the number of deer drives.

The way a deer drive works is a few hunters stand in a line at a designated place. Then another line of hunters, walking spitting distance apart will walk, as a line, towards the first group of hunters. All might carry guns, but those doing the walking will rarely see the deer that they are flushing out in front of them, and it will be the hunters on post that do most of the shooting. Much care must be taken to not shoot other hunters because many of them are out and it is difficult to tell where everyone is at any given time.

When deer are driven from their hiding places their path will often be a large arc. They seem to want to prefer to return to where they were, and to see whatever it is that drove them out.

Running shots at deer will be expected and hitting a fast moving target is always more difficult than hitting a stationary target.

One more thing to note about driving deer is that does will often make lots of noise when they are spooked. They will snort, and not make any effort to run away quietly. Does usually want to let all nearby deer know that there is danger around. Bucks are more likely to just try and disappear. Does will sometimes just try and disappear too, but if a deer is moving quietly it is most likely a buck.

Another deer hunting method is to walk around in the woods very slowly and quietly hoping to see a deer. I have tried this but have found it to be extremely ineffective and difficult. You are much better off stand hunting. When attempting this method you do not want to walk faster than around one step every ten minutes, or so I'm told. I'm no where near patient enough for that, and that would explain my poor results while attempting it (one miss with a muzzleloader).

Generally I find that even if you are sitting absolutely still a deer will know that you are around when you're on the ground and not too far away.

All of the above mentioned deer hunting methods are of most use while hunting with a gun. It is incredibly difficult to get into archery range while hunting any of those ways. Hitting a running deer, during a deer drive, with an arrow would be a near impossible feat; almost no one would even try it.'

The method of hunting deer most used today, and nearly exclusively by me, is stand hunting. The plan with stand hunting is to pick a good spot and then wait for the deer to arrive. The spot might be improved with bait, water, or food plots, but that is not always necessary.

Much like the tracker, a stand hunter needs to know the land. Deer need food, water, and cover. A stand hunter needs to know where all of those things are. Deer will spend their days in the cover and move to where there is food at dawn and dusk.

Ideally a stand hunter will have his stand located between the cover, parts of which are a deer's bedding area, and the food, and/or water. Putting your stand in the cover will drive the deer away from that cover and looking for cover somewhere else. Putting your stand directly over the food, or water, means that there will be times when there are so many deer around that you won't be able to move to shoot a deer. Deer are always looking out for danger and when you're over food, they may be lots of deer, and lots of deer noses, eyes, and ears looking out for trouble.

Stand hunting deer has lots of advantages. Hunting from a stand means that you'll rarely get lost, you get to hunt your own property, even if it is small, and you get to create and improve your own habitat. Its really the only way to hunt with a bow as well. (Unless your hunting skill vastly exceeds the author's, and if so, you'd not need to read a book like this.)

16

Stand Hunting

Each property is different, and each stand location will be different. But there are always lots of similarities among successful stand locations.

Deer prefer thick cover during daylight hours; that means hunting hours too. So, if you can look over a few hundred yards easily, then there won't be much cover for the deer to hide in. Take note of the thickest cover in your area. If you took my earlier advice to clear cut lots of trees, then after a few years of brush growth you should have a large area of thick cover that you never enter and where the deer will feel safe. Never enter your thickest cover. The more human scent and sounds that the deer sense there, the more likely they are to find somewhere else. Don't crowd your cover either; give the deer lots of room to feel safe.

Once you've located your cover you should take note of any deer trails that enter it. During the fall bucks will often rub their antlers on trees about two feet off of the ground. They will rub the bark off of the trees and these can be seen very easily.

You may even be able to use an internet maps' satellite view to zoom way in and see some deer trails. Don't expect to accomplish much from one of those maps, but they can be useful.

One of the best stand locations that I have ever found is where all trails in the area pass through one small clearing. No matter which trail you follow in the area you will pass through the little clearing.

Learning where deer enter a field may be as easy as finding where the most deer tracks are. The best time to look will be right after a rain or snow. The rain or snow will cover the old tracks and only the new ones will be seen.

Finding the most tracks may show you where deer enter a field, but the terrain itself should be able to tell you where the deer travel. Heavy cover near the north end of your field will tell you that the deer will enter the field at the north end. Put your stand between the thickest cover and the entrance point to the field.

Deer prefer cover to the open during hunting hours. Places where the cover narrows will be places where more deer pass through. These funnels will be a place where more deer will pass though than they would without the funnel.

Changes in elevation, even of only a foot, are also prime targets for deer activity. Deer like to be up higher and look around for danger, and even being a foot higher helps.

The best way to get a feel for where the deer prefer to travel is to watch them. And the best way to know where to put your stand is to hunt there and watch the deer. If you're very new to hunting, you may even go sit in a tree in the woods, without a weapon, before the season starts. Now that I have a bit of experience, I consider all of the deer I saw the previous season to select where I hang my treestands. Preseason scouting can be of great help to you new hunters, both for seeing how deer behave and where they are located.

Put your stand in a likely place and then hunt there, move the stand if you see all the deer in some other place. When you do see deer they will likely take the route that many deer will take in the future. Once you've hunted for a while you won't even need to see deer in order to tell where you want to hunt from. I can sit in a tree for a night and then decide that I don't want my stand here, I want it over there.

After deciding to move a stand, wait until the middle of the day to do so. Don't be moving around and making noise during the best hunting hours.

Determining the best stands by sitting in different stands throughout a hunting season is an effective way to learn the land, but you won't spend much time in the best spots. That may not be a problem because in a new place you won't likely know what the best place is immediately anyway.

Spending your first year hunting all sorts of places should give you several ideas for good stands. Unless the cover, food, and water situation changes a good spot is likely to be good for many years. You'll want to continue to improve your spots every year. Some you'll continue to use and some you'll stop using.

Spots will also be good at different times of the year. The best place to hunt will often be where the deer food is in its peak season. I recall one night where does came to me from all directions to eat the acorns that were falling from the nearby trees. Occasionally a few trees will drop lots of acorns all at once and that's where you'll want to be. Your apple trees will all likely drop their apples at once too. The plants in your food plots will all hit their peak at different times too. It would be good to take note of all of your plant growth and which plants are planted where and when they become favored by deer.

Trail cameras, or game cameras, can be a help in determining where some spots are, or where the biggest bucks are located too.

When you get to a new piece of property ask yourself: where's the cover? Where's the food? When the deer walk from the cover to the food, where will they be?

17

Treestand Styles

There are several types of stand from which you can hunt deer. The simplest type requires no equipment at all. Sit on a rock or a log, and maybe pile some brush around you. This can be an good way to hunt for deer, but it is easily the least effective type of deer stand. Although, this might be the stand you use if you want to sit on the top of a hill and look down. If this is the case, then you may not want to be any higher.

Deer know that you're there when you're on the ground. If you want to shoot the first deer you see, with a gun but not a bow, then the ground is okay, but you'll need to be in some sort of treestand if your goal is bucks, or big bucks.

At one time people nailed boards into trees for stands. These were notable for rotting or having the tree grow and having the hunter fall out to great injury or death. There are many fine stands for sale, don't hunt from boards nailed into trees.

Another type of ground stand is to use a tent, or ground blind. Ground blinds are very inexpensive and should be the preferred option for those of you who do not want to leave the ground. A ground blind has the advantage that nearly all of your movement, and scent, will be concealed. Apparently, turkeys are likely to notice hunters moving from the more traditional treestands, and ground blinds are the way to go. They also provide shelter from wind and precipitation.

They do have a large disadvantage, however, you can see a lot more the higher you are, and so sitting on the ground gives you limited visibility. And a large tent on the ground is likely to be avoided by deer.

You may want to build your own ground blind. Many people build boxes and sit in them. They have the same advantages and more disadvantages to the tent style ground blind. A box will be a permanent structure and you will not be able to move it. Being made out of wood, it will also rot and acquire bugs and mice.

Lots and lots of hunters in Wisconsin, including the author, have built elevated boxes. These have all of the advantages, and disadvantages, listed above plus they are elevated. This covers the biggest disadvantage of ground blinds.

There are lots of disadvantages to hunting from an elevated box, but having one on your property means that you have a place to hunt when the weather would keep you from staying out otherwise. In the coldest regions of deer territory, elevated boxes provide a place to hunt where you can keep a heater or anything else that you need to stay out in the cold. If you have limited mobility, then an elevated box with stairs might be the only way that you hunt from an elevated position.. if you smoke a box helps to contain the scent. If you can't sit still, a box helps to hide some of the movement.

An elevated box can be built however you want. Add TV satellite dishes, heaters, refrigerators, etc. I don't actually recommend adding any of that stuff because it will distract you from the task at hand.

A blind to buy is one that is easy to move out into the woods, is quiet when it gets there, has small windows to cover your movement, and is made of quality components. Lock-N-Load Blinds (lock-n-load.net) are easily moveable due to their extreme lightweight, stay solid when put together and are made from good stuff that won't fade in the sun. A five minute assembly, with no tools required, is quite a feature too.

If you do make one yourself, then you should make the windows as small as possible. The more that you are covered the more of your movement will be concealed. Big windows do not block much wind either. Some people like glass, or plastic, windows to keep the weather out. I would prefer not to have windows to move when I want to shoot a deer. If I wanted to be comfortable, I wouldn't be hunting when it is cold, or rainy. And that extra movement necessary to open the window is likely to be the difference between shooting a deer and having him see you first.

A tower has its uses, but many deer will prefer to avoid big boxes out in the woods; particularly the big bucks, and particularly the first year that it is up. A tripod is a more mobile version of a tower. A tripod can be very useful in some instances. If there are no large trees around and you want the best viewing area possible, then a tripod will put up in the air. And a tripod is not just a large box that the deer may want to avoid. If you use a tripod, make sure that some brush or something is behind you so that you are not silhouetted against the sky. Tripods don't conceal much movement and are therefore not as good as blinds when you are hunting with a gun and may have long shots.

Being higher is generally better. Twelve feet is about as low as tripods go, and some go up to twenty feet.

The things to look for in a tripod are: height, sturdiness, and being able to swivel your seat silently. Tripods are more mobile than towers, but will still require at least two people to move while it is assembled. Aluminum tripods will creak in the cold, and are therefore worse than useless in the cold.

Another type of deer stand is a ladder stand. This is a stand style preferred by hunters who aren't as mobile, or agile, as they might be. They are ladders with a platform and seat on top which you lean against a tree and attached with straps.

Ladder stands can be wide enough for one person, or two. Their ladders can be wide or narrow as well. I do not recommend the narrow ladder version; they may be lighter, but you'll be forced to climb them like a fashion model walks the runway. This is uncomfortable for me to do, despite being in reasonable shape and in my twenties, and its particularly difficult with hunting clothes and boots on.

Ladder stands, with wide ladders, are easy to climb and can go up trees that are oddly shaped or very full of branches.

I don't care for commercially available ladder stands because they always seem to be wobbly. The almost all have arm rests as well. Arm rests make a stand more comfortable, but get in the way of some shooting angles. This is especially true while hunting with a bow. They are generally heavy and very noisy to move to where you want them. Two people can put one up, but may be very hesitant to do so if they have done it before; and that's with a one person variety. Plan on needing three people to put ladder stands up.

A two person ladder stand is probably the stand to use if you want to hunt with a young son or daughter. Two people with minimal presence in an elevated spot is the way to go. A box tower would also work but they require much more work to put up (except for the Lock-N-Load blinds) and are more likely to be avoided by the deer.

The last time I participated in moving a ladder stand I vowed never to buy one, and hopefully never move one again. Putting all that weight on the top of a narrow ladder is just asking for trouble when you move it. I am surprised that I have not been injured when moving one. And yet ladder stands seem to be the most popular kind of deer hunting stand; I note however not the most popular kind among good deer hunters.

Climbing stands are the most mobile type of treestand. Hunting on public land will nearly require that you hunt from a climber. Other stand types are meant to stay up permanently and that is often illegal on public land. Even if permanent stands are not illegal you'll need to lock them in and be annoyed when other hunters use them.

Climbing stands come in a few varieties. Some are like lounge chairs and a probably very comfortable... and difficult to shoot from. Others are just platforms with a strap around the tree. Most climbing stands will come with a seat which will be a smaller version of the floor platform.

A climbing stand will require a very straight tree with no branches for the first twenty feet. This restriction will greatly limit the number of trees available for you to sit in. But their mobility is unquestionable. If you can afford only one hunting stand, then a climber will be the one that you want to get. (Lone Wolf Hand Climber $380)

Another benefit of using a climbing stand is that your abs will really get a good workout. It is not difficult to use one, but the repeated climbing action will work your abs quite well.

One more deer stand style is a chain on, or strap on, or hang on. This will consist of a stand and a ladder or some other form of steps to get to the stand.

The next chapter will be about hang on stands but many of the points will relate to the other stand styles too.

18

Hang On Treestands

Treestands are a collection of trade offs in design inputs and decisions. The good ones are elegantly simple in accomplishing the task. The poorly designed ones are pieces of crap.

Hang on, chain on, or strap on treestands are a platform, a seat and upright bars between the two that are held together by a cable or chain on each side. A chain or strap will hold the stand to the tree.

This style of stand is the best for hunting deer as effectively and efficiently as possible. They are better than the towers, tripods, and ladders because they are more discreet. They are better than ground blinds and boxes because they are elevated. Hang on stands are better than climbers because they are much quieter to use and you won't need to carry it in for each hunt, nor find a straight tree without branches on the bottom half.

The two downsides of hang on treestands are the need to put them up before hunting and the need to have several of them. Last season my father and I had 17 chain on stands in place at one point in the season. (And it still wasn't enough.)

When you have all of your stands up, you'll be able to walk to one of many treestands and then climb up it and hunt. No need to carry one in each time, and you should have one for every wind direction..

There are two parts you need to buy in order hunt from a chain on treestand: a stand and a ladder or other means to reach the stand. "A ladder," in this case, is not an extension ladder or stepladder, but a purpose built hunting item. "Climbing sticks" will be the search term that you use to find them.

There are a few things that you should know about a chain on stand before selecting one to buy. Many of these points will be helpful for picking out other stand types as well.

The ideal chain on treestand will: 1) have a large floor 2) weigh less than 16 pounds 3) use ratchet straps, or a chain, to fasten to the tree 4) have a seat that is comfortable without a foam pad (squirrel bedding as I call the foam seat cushions) 5) be reasonably priced 6) have a footrest 7) a mesh floor 8)and, this should go without mentioning, be of a quality construction and support your weight.

Imagine that you are fifteen feet up a tree. Do you prefer a large platform to stand on or a small one? Without question, the bigger the floor, the better it is. That's not just for comfort, but also because a larger floor means that you will be better able to move to shoot from awkward positions.

I am not going to recommend a particular size. Understand that bigger is better, until it gets to the point that it is too heavy and cumbersome to safely hang. Remember what I said about design trade off decisions?

Bigger is better when the stand is in the tree and you are hunting from it. You also need to consider carrying it to the tree, putting it up , and taking it down. Twenty pounds is not a lot of weight. Carrying twenty pounds of awkward metal up a tree with branches is not even a little bit fun.

Some treestands sold weigh 25-30 pounds. A new treestand that you will see selling for much less than $100 will weigh more than twenty pounds. If a sales guy tries to sell you a hang on treestand that weighs more than twenty pounds, laugh in his face.

Many of you who read this are going to buy a certain $60 treestand that weighs something like 26 pounds. When you are putting them up, think of me and my advising you to not buy one of those!

On second thought, heavy treestands are great! Coincidentally, I have two for sale: real cheap.

There are even some treestands with armrests, cushioned seats, cushioned back rests, etc, etc, etc. Those stands weigh so much you may as well build a tree house instead. And those armrests and everything will only get in the way. If you want to be as comfortable as possible, then don't go deer hunting, or even outside.

When I shot my most recent buck with a bow one of my dad's friends came over to help find it. He saw my stand with its small metal seat and said that I must have been very uncomfortable. I pointed out that you can be comfortable or shoot deer, pick one. If you want to be comfortable, then I recommend a big cushioned seat, in front of a TV, in the heat or air conditioning.

That's not to say comfort is unimportant, because you'll not stay out and fidget more if you are uncomfortable, but all that extra stuff will get in your way when the time comes to shoot a deer.

There are several ways that a hang on stand will be attached to a tree. One way is a chain and a hook. This is the safest version because a chain is not likely to break. Chains are also noisy and you should paint the chain so that it is not shiny.

For future reference, if you paint a hunting product, then paint it brown, black, or green; or a mix of all three.

Chains are strong but difficult to attach tightly. Ratchet straps are the only way to attach a stand, or ladder, to a tree tightly. You might think that other types of seat belt straps and buckled straps are okay, but they are never as tight as you think that they are. Ratchet straps attach things tightly, but they wear out in the sun and weather. (Also: squirrels may chew them.) Replace them every two years, or at any time that you question their strength.

Replace all straps for hang on treestands and ladders with chains or ratchet straps. Don't bother with anything else. Don't be cheap with safety.

Many of you will ignore the previous paragraph and use whatever straps came with your stand or ladder. When you fall from your tree, remember that I told you not to use anything other than a chain or ratchet strap.

A tree stand's seat is an important part. Trying to shoot a deer will mean many hours of time spent in a tree, and you cannot stand forever. Later we will look at the advantages and disadvantages to sitting and standing while hunting.

The ideal seat should be a little bit too high to be really comfortable. I know that sounds strange, but you want to sit on the seat and not into the seat. If the seat is a little higher, it is easy to stand with minimal effort and movement. Also seats that sit on, not in, are easier to turn to the right (assuming you are right handed) than some of those great big comfortable seats that you sit deep into.

There are, basically, two types of seats. One type is a metal, or wood, flat surface. The other type has three, or four, metal bars and some sort of soft materiel between the bars. There are good versions, and bad versions of each type.

The best kind of flat seat has a full metal mesh welded onto the top of a solid frame. This type of seat is fine to sit on, although when it is cold out, the metal will be cold. A foam cushion is often added to the top to distance your butt from the cold and to be soft.

The bad type of flat seat has the metal ring, but no mesh on top. This type of seat is meant only to be used with the foam cushion. You will be immensely uncomfortable without the cushion. I would not forgo hunting because I forgot the cushion, but I would not enjoy my hunt without it, and I'll fidget more and consider leaving early.

A treestand's seat cushion makes the seat a lot more comfortable, and is almost required when it is cold out. But the cushion has lots of problems too. Leaving the cushion in the stand means that it will absorb water when there is precipitation and squirrels will tear them up. Taking the cushion down every time means that you need to remember to carry it in every time that you hunt, and you will make Velcro noises when entering and leaving your stand. You will also need to remember which cushion goes with each stand.

Seat cushions are not great while you are hunting anyway. While hunting from a treestand you will be a ways up a tree. The last thing that you will want is a seat that moves around and the cushion will move around. The cushion will also mean that the seat is thicker than it needs to be. This means that when you fold it up against the tree, giving you more room to stand up, it will not fold tight against the tree.

All of the problems with seat cushions are minor annoyances. But they are annoyances. Seat cushions are less than ideal for maximum "huntability."

Do note that I am in my twenties, and if I were older I may be unwilling to hunt a treestand without something softer than metal to sit on.

The second style of treestand seat has three, or four, metal bars and some sort of materiel hanging between them.

The Family Traditions tree stands uses seat belt material, but is made of aluminum that creaks like mad in the cold. The Ol' Man The Roost treestands use a mesh system that is comfortable. Other stands like the newer Gorilla stands and the Millennium stands have large comfortable mesh seats. My father prefers these sorts of seats for all day hunts, but personally I prefer to sit on the hard metal mesh.

You will want to avoid the stands that have all four sides of the seat surrounded by a metal bar. The three bared seats (sides and back) avoid having the bar across the front which will cut off circulation in your legs. Cutting off circulation will make you uncomfortable, which will make you fidget, which will be noticed by deer. Do not buy a treestand that has a seat of four metal bars with the seat hanging inside them. Buy a stand with the bar missing from the front.

We're not done looking at seats because the seat shape can affect weather or not you get a chance to shoot a deer. The ideal seat shape is small and round, and without arm rests. There is a range of angles from which you can shoot a gun or bow without moving your butt. There is a much wider range of angles that you can shoot if you can turn on your seat. Large and square seats prevent you from turning. Seats that you sit in rather than on are not good for turning around on. Armrests prevent you from turning. And seat cushions are more inclined to slide rather than turn. When I am turning I prefer to sit on something that will not move. Seats that rotate will get stuck at some point and/ or make noise.

A small round seat that you sit on, rather than in, gives you the most freedom to turn and means that you will have more opportunities to shoot at deer.

A footrest on a treestand would seem to be a minor feature. You will not miss not having a footrest if you never sit in a stand that has one. I went around ten years being perfectly comfortable in treestands without footrests. But once you hunt from a stand that has one you will miss it when you don't have one. Some treestands include footrests, some offer them as options, and some have none at all. Buy the optional footrest if it is an option, but don't be too concerned about it.

Mesh floors on treestands have been called the greatest innovation in treestands by some deer hunters. A deer that looks up and sees a black shape will be more inclined to avoid that unnatural presence than he would a stand that allows some of the sky to be seen through it. Don't do something like add a square of carpet to the floor of a stand. I've seen guys do this and it means a big black, unnatural shape a deer can see when it looks up.

Obviously you want to buy treestands that are well made and are capable of holding you up. I don't recall ever seeing a new treestand that was not of at least reasonable quality. One thing I will say is that stands, or any hunting product, with the name of some TV show on them does not all of a sudden make that product high quality. [insert eye roll]

Hang on treestands are mostly rated as safe for hunters who weigh less than 300 pounds. I applaud those of you who weigh 300 pounds and want to climb trees, but I would recommend getting a ladder stand, a tripod, or building a tower instead.

Probably the first hang on tree stand to get it all right was Paul Brunner's original Screaming Eagle stands. These were steel chain on stands with mesh decks and small seats that were a little higher than most other stands. My father and I both agree that the best commercial stand ever made was the original Gorilla King Kong stands. Sadly, these are no longer available. The last few stands that we have purchased have been the large Lone Wolf stands.

Having a hang on treestand is good but you'll need some means of reaching it. There are several variations for climbing ladders. One variation is a one inch metal tube that has various sections that stack on top of each other and has steps sticking out from either side. Another variation has the central tube, but each section is separately attached to the tree. Another variation has the metal tubes on the outside with the steps in the middle and each section stacks on another. The last variation has the bars on the outside, rungs in the middle and each section is independent.

Aside from those ladder sections, you may also elect to use the metal screw-in steps. Screw-in steps was the old way of climbing a tree. I don't like them because of the holes you need to put into the trees, the difficulty in doing so, and the problems that may arise if you cut down a tree with metal steps in it. Bring your cordless drill if you plan on using screw-in steps.

The one great advantage of the screw-in steps is the ability to put them up in any order up any tree. Hunters used to use screw in steps to reach their stands. Imagine hitting a forgotten one with a chainsaw later. I also know a guy who fell and has a scar in his side where he was hanging from the tree with a screw in step in his side. I'd pass on the screw in steps.

The ladder sections require a straighter tree than the screw-in steps. And the independent step sections require a less straight tree than the sections than the ladder sections that stack.

Ladder sections with outside rails and inside rungs are very narrow; room only for one foot in a medium, or smaller, weight boot. I do not like these kinds of ladders because of how little foot space that they provide. I do not like climbing a tree like how a fashion model walks the runway, especially in big boots.

This leaves us with ladders that have their steps out either side of a central post. These ladders may be independent of each other or stack. The independent ones can go up more irregular trees. The ones that stack are much easier to climb. You can climb a stacked stick in the dark, but you will need to look for each step with a non-stacking climbing stick.

The last thing to decide on is whether the steps are even on each side or only alternate. The steps on your ladder are much easier to climb when the steps stick out from each side at each height rather than only alternate. This can be a big point. Having steps out each side at every interval are massively easier to climb than those with alternating steps. Climbing sticks that have steps on both sides at each step also makes hanging stands much safer.

As for specific hang on treestand recommendations, I will point out that I have used many hang-ons in the past; including: Screaming Eagle, a variety from Big Game, a variety from Rivers Edge, Lone Wolf Alpha Hang On II, Lone Wolf Assault II, Family Traditions, Twisted Timber, the original Gorilla Kong, King Kong, & King Kong Silverback, the newer Gorilla King Kong (two varieties), Ol' Man the Roost, Ol' Man the Roost aluminum, and three of which I do not know the names of. I have not tried a Muddy treestand (if they made the seat the way I like the seats to be they would be excellent, but I don't like the seats). I don't care for the floors on the Summits (think of all the light they block from above), and the Comfort Zone stands do not have the seats that I like either.

I have hunted from all sorts of hang on treestands and I'll say that the best hang on treestand being made today is the Lone Wolf Alpha Hang-On II, at $250. The best small stand being made today is the Lone Wolf Assault, also not cheap. If you need more comfort than one of the stands with the mesh seats might be the best choice for you.

The original Gorilla King Kong was darn near perfect. The newer King Kong was almost as good. The quarter century old Screaming Eagle was very good too. But the only near ideal stands left on the market are those made by Lone Wolf. If I could, I would replace every stand we own with an original Gorilla King Kong. Sadly, those stands are no longer available.

19

Picking Your Spot

If you are new to hunting deer, then you'll need to know where to specifically hunt. The only way to determine where you should hunt is to walk around the property that you plan to hunt and look for places.

A good place to start looking is to walk along edges. Walk along the edges of fields, marshes, lawns, roads, fences, streams, ditches, brushy areas, and so on. Anywhere that you have deer and an edge to differentiate two pieces of land types, or an edge over which deer must cross, you should be able to find deer trails.

Trails should be easy enough to recognize. They'll be the lines on the ground with only bare dirt, or where all the weeds or brush has been moved aside. When you have only a few inches of snow on the groud, the bigger deer trails will be the lines where there is no snow on the ground.

Deer will walk all over the place but they will prefer some places to others. Once you've walked around enough you'll notice the places where the deer usually cross ditches and enter fields.

Find those places and you could do worse than hunt there. There are likely to be trails that run along those edges too. A trail parallel and a trail perpendicular to an edge is a trail intersection which should be a good spot.

Then you can follow the trails around to find deer beds, food, and other trails.

If you are new to hunting, then find the edges, then the trails then pick your trees. A considerable amount of though will need to go into placing those stands.

The first thing is to select a tree in the general area that you want. A climbing treestand will require a nearly straight tree devoid of branches. A hang on stand, with ladder section steps needs a straight tree, and a hang on stand with screw in steps can go up nearly any tree.

The tree should be at least nine inches in diameter for any style of stand. I've tried going up trees that are as small as five inches in diameter, but they are way too wobbly and you can't get up high enough. And then when you sit in them too often the tree will lean forwards, which is amazingly uncomfortable. The first buck I shot over a food plot was from a great tree that now leans forward, I suspect because I sat in it too often when it was too small for me to sit in.

The tree should be alive. Lots of trees will remain standing for years after they die, but you will not know when they will fall, and you won't want to be up a dead tree when it does decide to fall. Adding your weight fifteen feet up a dead tree probably does not help the stability of the tree either.

When using a hang on stand, or a ladder stand, you may want to go up a tree that has lots of branches. Branches are good for cover. A big part of stand hunting is to be concealed, and being surrounded by branches is a great help in being concealed.

When my dad and I look for stand locations we argue the merits of more branches or less. He prefers to be surrounded by more branches in order to be more concealed. I prefer fewer branches because branches get in the way of shooting. Branches are particularly troublesome when hunting with a bow.

Once you put your stand in the tree you'll want to sit in it to make sure that it is in solidly and you'll want to trim some branches. Many branches may need to be cut from the stand. While sitting pretend like you are drawing your bow and then cut the branches that would seem to be in the way. Then stand and cut the branches that would seem to be in the way. Cut more than you think you need to. The branch you leave may be the one between you and a 130 B&C buck.

A deer that is behind you cannot be shot while sitting, you'll need to stand in order to turn around enough. This will affect your branch trimming.

Ideally you will sit in your new stand and direct someone else to cut branches that you cannot reach from your stand.

The somewhat new saws on sticks are extremely helpful. But a cheap one, as in less than, say, $70, are worthless. A good saw on a stick (Hooeyman) will allow you to reach and remove very few select small branches rather than whole large branches or whole trees.

You'll need to decide whether to put your stand up a tree full of branches or a tree with fewer branches, and you'll need to decide whether to trim more or less branches. But usually there will be a tree that is obvious for a stand and you'll need to live with the number of branches that it has. The location is what is most important, not the number branches.

Trees with branches are usually what you will have to work with, but don't overlook trees with multiple trunks or clumps of trees. My Favorite Tree (capitol letters for a proper noun) has two trunks that split at the ground, another big tree to my left, another double to my right, and a another one behind. None of these trees have many branches at less than fifty feet off the ground, which is good for shooting, and yet the number of tree trunks on all sides means that I am never an obvious thing for the deer to see. There is always another tree trunk behind me.

There are all sorts of trees that you may sit in, consider the best spot and fit that tree to your hunting. We may prefer hang on tree stands to go up straight trees and a straight stick steps to go up and down, but it is good to have a stand meant for going up angled or crooked trees and some screw in steps. It would be a shame to not hunt the best tree because you don't have the equipment to do so. Twisted Timber makes a stand for angled trees.

The two most important things in staying out of a deer's sight are to not move and not be silhouetted against the sky. You can guess where the deer will be and then you will want a tree full of branches behind you. If you are in a heavily wooded area this will not be a concern, but you will not want to be in the only tall tree in the area either. If your only tree option does make you silhouetted, then you will want to trim fewer branches away, and maybe add some branches behind you.

Once you have selected your tree you will want to decide on which direction to point it. This requires more thought than you might think.

The angle of your treestand is very important. The biggest buck that my dad has ever seen from a tree was straight behind him and he was not able to twist around the tree enough to get a shot. Smaller trees are easier to twist around, but they are less stable.

First decide about where you think that most of the deer will be. From there we will arrange the stand.

You do not want to point your stand straight at where you expect the deer to be. You will want to angle your stand to the right of that place. (Reverse this, and the following directions, if you are left handed.)

Your left side (if you are right handed) will be what faces the deer when you shoot. Shooting a bow and a rifle change the angles a bit, but you will be easily able to shoot from 8 to 12 without moving below the waist. You will want to have the left front (away from the tree) stand corner to face where you think that the deer will be. You may want to error on the side of the front of the stand facing the deer, because you will spend most of your time looking straight ahead and you are more likely to see deer that are in front of you.

You want the deer to be in front of you to see them and to your left to shoot them.

One more thing to know is that you cannot, with a bow, shoot a deer that is facing you our pointing straight away. You need to have the deer's side facing you. So you do not want your stand on a trail so that the deer that walk the trail are straight on or straight away from you.

Many trees will not give you options for the ideal angle. Other trees' big branches will often prevent your ideal treestand angle. Do what you can. Cut what you think you need to.

One more important thing to think about is the lean of the tree. A tree with a stand in it can go straight up, or it can lean away from where your stand faces. Even slight lean forwards can make a sit become very uncomfortable. You will not enjoy feeling like you are leaning over the edge of your stand. Leaning to one side, a little, is not too bad, but leaning forwards at all, or to a side a lot is unacceptable.

For the most part, you pick your ideal stand location, then pick the best tree that is there. The trees available will decide how you face your stand, how high you go up, and how many branches that you need to trim.

Pick your spot. Then take the most appealing tree available from which you can shoot to your left from, and then improve what you can.

Hunting from your new stand will show you a lot. Once you hunt from it you may want to point it in a different direction or change trees altogether, and you may want to remove more branches. Move it if you want to, but wait until the next day, don't move your stand around during your prime hunting hours.

20

Hanging Stands

After you have selected your tree it is time to put your stand up. I realize that much of this chapter may seem too simple to be necessary to be included, but there can be much struggle in setting treestands up. And some of you may not know how to do it.

A climbing treestand is carried in each time that you hunt. The way a climbing treestand will work is as follows:

Walk to your selected tree with your weapon and your stand.

Put the strap around the tree so that the floor of the stand is at a large angle. The front of the stand should be significantly higher than the back, which is near the tree. A tree gets narrower the higher it gets and the angle of the stand will change as it climbs higher. You absolutely do not want your stand to lean forwards once it is up. That will give you the sensation of thinking that you are about to fall out of your tree at any moment, and in a climber your sensation may be accurate.

The seat, if you use it, will go just above the floor at a similar angle. Your abs will get a better workout with the seat and the tree bark will be rough on your arms without the seat. But the seat will not fold up, and out of the way, so you will not be able to stand up, which is better in some cases.

Then you will tie a rope from your weapon to your stand. (Thicker ropes are less likely to get tangled.) Don't load your gun until it is up the tree. Shooting yourself by pulling your gun up with a rope would be a stupid way to die, and its been done.

Climb atop the floor and then put your arms on the seat with your elbows at your sides. Or, without the seat, hug the tree.

Put your feet between the strap and floor, or under the foot straps if the stand has them.

With your legs and abs tilt the floor so the front, behind you at this point, is higher, and the stand is lose. Lift the floor a ways then un-tilt the floor.

Tilt the seat in the same way and then stand and re-tilt at a higher point. Or let go of the tree, stand up, and re-hug at a higher point.

Repeat until you are fifteen to twenty feet up.

This is not terribly difficult. I could do it at thirteen with no problems. Although I thought, at the time, that ten feet up was plenty high enough.

Make sure that the stand is in snug at its point for hunting.

Then turn and sit down and pull your weapon up with the rope. Don't let the rope swing in the breeze, the deer may notice, and avoid that. Put the rope in your pocket while you are hunting.

A ladder stand goes up as follows: with a total of two or three guys, carry in the ladder and its sections. Try not to make too much noise, but lots of noise will be unavoidable.

Assemble the sections; this will require lots of room.

Arrange the base so that it is around six feet away from the tree base, and have one guy hold the base in place.

The other two guys will walk the stand up and into the tree.

There may be some loose straps to tie the stand on while climbing it halfway up. Then use ratchet straps to secure the top of the stand to the tree.

There may also be a bar that is meant to extend from the tree to the ladder halfway up its height.

Tripods are carried into place, as a whole, or in sections, and then stood up into place.

Hang on treestands and their accompanying steps are installed as follows:

After arriving at the tree, untangle the step straps and make sure that the straps are set for the size of the tree that you are about to climb. You do not want to adjust the straps when you are part ways up a tree.

Note that ratchet straps and chains are the only good options. Use nothing else.

There are two types of climbing sticks, those that stack on top of one another, and those that are independent. In both cases they will have a v-shaped piece of metal that faces the tree. First the stacking ones:

Determine where you want the stand to face and then put the first stick section about 90 degrees to one side. Loosely tighten the first strap, leaving some slack in the strap. Because trees are not perfectly straight, the first stick will often be at an angle too severe for you to put the second stick on if the first one is on tightly.

Put the second stick, and strap, on and make it a little tighter.

Do the same for the next stick, or two, and then tighten them as tight as you can.

Then climb down and tighten the bottom two straps.

For the non-stacking sticks the procedure is the same, except you do not need to put them in a straight line. They are much easier to climb when they are in-line with each other. These will slide down the tree slightly so you should step on each one to make that little slide when you are prepared for it to happen.

Climbing a stacking stick can be done incredibly easily without even the need for light. Independent steps will require that you look for each foot position before you step on it. But independent climbing sticks give you the ability to climb irregular trees.

Once your sticks are in place you will set up the stand on the ground, so that you don't need to do any adjusting while up the tree. When carrying your stand up you will really appreciate having a light stand, having the stick steps in a line, and having a stick with steps on each side at every rung level (as opposed to alternating steps). Carrying a stand up means that you will be using one hand and two feet to climb and will be about as physically demanding as stand hunting gets.

You can climb to the top and then haul the stand up with a rope, but I find that a stand hanging from a rope is hard to control. A stand hanging in this way will swing into the climbing stick, and be noisy, and it will catch on every branch that it can on the way up. It is generally easier to carry it up with one hand and only have the other available for climbing.

At the top of the stick you will be holding the stand up with one hand, hanging onto the tree with your other hand, throwing the strap around the tree with another hand, and then catching and hooking the strap to the stand with your fourth hand. Have fun with that part.

The sticks that have steps at every height, instead of alternating, have the great advantage of giving you the option you hook one knee around the top step while you attach the stand. This will leave you with two free hands. Sticks that have alternating steps will require much more difficult balancing in order to attach the stand. You won't really ever have both hands free if you have a climbing step variety other than the stacking with steps out each side variety.

At this point, I'll mention that some hunters use a safety harness which is attached to a rope above them. I've never tried one for climbing a tree, but you should use one for safety, and so that I can point here if someone tries to sue me after falling without one.

You'll want the floor of your stand at around the same height as the top of the climbing stick, at about 90 degrees to one side.

Once the strap is around the tree the stand will slide down a little as you tighten the strap. Like I said in an earlier chapter, chains will not break, but they are noisy and will never be as tight as you might like.

You may push the stand down to tighten the stand, and with some stands the floor tilts with the "v" that touches the tree. Lift the floor, push the stand down, and then straighten the floor for a stand that is as tight as you can get it. (This will especially be the case if you don't remove your stand each year while the tree grows.)

Adding an additional ratchet strap to your stand is always a good idea for tightness and as a backup safety measure. I believe the correct number of ratchets is however many you think you need, plus one.

Climbing with the aid of tree branches may sound like a good idea, but they are likely to bend and break. The closest that I've ever come to falling out of a tree was when I grabbed a branch that held for just long enough for me to hug the tree with my other arm. Had it broken any sooner I would have fallen off.

I recommend busting all small or dead branches off any tree you climb. If you start to fall you'll be better off grabbing to hug the tree rather than grabbing a dead branch. And if you see a branch you'll grab it without thinking of how alive it is, bust it off, and then fall.

Whatever stand that you use, you are advised to remove it at least every year. Trees grow and the longer you leave your stand up the harder it will be to remove the stand. You should carry a knife with you while removing the stands in case you need to cut straps. Good luck removing chains that have had their trees grow around them.

Straps are recommended by their manufacturers to be replaced every two years. I don't know that the exact best age to replace them is, but replace any straps that have begun to fray.

This chapter may have been a bit too obvious, but you should now be able to put each style of stand up with full knowledge of how to do it.

You'll learn a lot from hunting in a new stand for a night. Move it, or rotate it, afterwords, if you want to. But don't move the stand during peak hunting hours, no matter how much you may want to move the stand "right now."

I realize that I have repeated that you should not move a stand during peak hours repeatedly, but when a stand is not where I want it, my hunt will often be spent with me not being able to think of anything else.

21

Hunting Clothing

Hunting clothing is an important part of your hunting experience. If you are not comfortable while hunting you will fidget more, which deer will notice and they will avoid you. The less comfortable you are the more you will want to end your hunts early and you will not be as encouraged to hunt as often as you should.

The hunting clothing that you need will depend on the temperature, precipitation, and your local laws.

Check your local laws for your clothing requirements. Some states require the use of some amount of fluorescent orange clothing, and some require you to wear a certain amount of white. My state of Wisconsin requires a certain percentage of orange during firearm seasons, and is one of two states that still require the wearing of a back tag.

My clothing recommendation is to have a light brown camouflage coat and pants and then add and remove layers underneath, and add and remove an orange vest when the laws change with the different seasons (archery vs. firearm).

One point that lots of people don't seem to understand is that deer eyes are different from people eyes. You can look in any hunting magazine and see advertisements for camouflage clothing that is really hard to differentiate from the surrounding trees. But advertising has edited pictures and is irrelevant anyway because deer eyes are different from people eyes.

All sorts of animals have different sorts of eyes. No one thinks that an owl's eyes work the same as a mouse's, for example.

Deer are crepuscular. They are most active at dawn and dusk. These are low light conditions. In order to see the deer's eyes are good at collecting all available light but they do not see color very well.

Next time you see a deer notice the white ring around its eyes. It occurred to me last hunting season that this probably works exactly the opposite of the eye black football players wear. Football players wear eye black beneath their eyes to reduce the amount of light reflected into their eyes. Football fields are well light and too much light is tiring on eyes. Deer have white rings around their eyes to reflect as much light as possible into their eyes. This is very useful in low light conditions, but not as useful when your headlights overwhelm deer eyes and they sometimes freeze while they are blinded by too much light, such as in headlights.

So, deer see well in low light but they don't see color well.

I suspect that you could wear light pink and dark purple and be as well camouflaged as someone wearing light brown, dark brown, and green. However, hunting clothing is colored to sell itself to people, so it is designed to look camouflaged to people's eyes.

This is the case with fishing lures too. The variety of colors is mostly unnecessary. The difference is negligible between any two dark or any two light colors for most fish. But an attractive color is more likely to be sold than one that is less attractive, or boring

Mossy Oak and Realtree are the two main brands of camouflage sold today. Both are fine and I couldn't care less which brand my clothing has. A quality hunting coat or pants will likely have one of those two brands so that is what you will probably get. I can't be bothered to go and look at my coat and pants to see which camouflage pattern they have, it doesn't matter and both are fine. (Realtree says "Realtree" all over the pattern in small letters, and a Mossy Oak item will have the Mossy Oak logo somewhere on it.)

My dad says that he wears different patterns between his coat and pants: leafy camo pants and a bare branches coat, to confuse the deer, and to be amusing.

While deer cannot differentiate between camouflage patterns, they can differentiate between shades of colors. Think of a black and white movie. Everything is black, white, or gray. This is more like what a deer sees.

In this case you don't want to be all black, all white, or all gray. And solid shapes are unnatural. In the case of treestands a stand with a solid floor in one color will look out of place in nature. There are no straight lines or solid colors in nature. You want to have an irregular shape in a variety of colors.

There is probably a difference between light camouflage patterns and dark ones though. Match your surroundings as you can, but don't worry too much about it.

Many deer hunters in Wisconsin have solid orange outfits for the firearm season. They would be better served by having a camoflage orange pattern rather than a solid orange one when we are legally required to wear a certain amount of orange. A large area of one solid color looks out of place in nature, particularly if that color is fluorescent.

On the other hand, lots of deer get killed by guys wearing 100% fluorescent orange. This may lead us to believe that sitting still and quietly, while not smelling is more important that what color your clothes are. Many of those guys also smoke and talk on their phones while in trees and still shoot deer. So maybe this whole book is a waste and you can do whatever and it will work...on occasion.

There are also white camoflage patterns for hunting in the snow. You might end up with an orange coat for the firearm season, a white one for the snowy times of the year, and a brown camoflage one for the early part of the season. If I hunted where it was snowy for most of the deer season, I'd probably have a white camoflage pattern. But I hunt up trees and much of the hunting season, here in Wisconsin, occurs without snow. And the snow is usually on the ground when my brown camoflage is well matched to the brown trees around me.

The specific colors are not all that important, but the fading that occurs from washing your camouflage is. Some things are brighter than others. Trees and leaves and grasses are not bright, they are dully colored. Non hunters want brightly colored clothing. No one shows off by being dull.

Standard laundry detergent is designed to enhance the brightness of clothing. You will want to minimize the washing of hunting clothing. Buy a hunting specific laundry detergent which won't brighten, and use a UV killer to dullen your camouflage's colors. Hunting specific laundry detergents have the added benefit of not smelling like whatever the other detergents smell like.

What I recommend is having a medium weight camouflaged coat, and then adding layers underneath when it is cold and adding an orange camoflage vest when the law requires it.

Obviously if you hunt deer in places where it is warm during the season you're better off getting camouflage long sleeve t-shirts rather than coats. There are usually a few days of the season that I wish that I had one of those.

Hunting in warm weather means that you are more likely to sweat, which deer will smell, this means that you should find some scent absorbing clothing to reduce your sweat smells.

There are two main scent reducing hunting clothing companies: Scent Lok (scentlok.com) and Scent Shield (scentshield.com). Those two companies make hunting clothing, detergents, deodorants, scent killing clothing spray and/ or other scent reducing products.

I would bet that one brand is better than the other at limiting smells, but I don't have any idea which it is and I don't care.

Expect to pay $50-100 for non scent proof hunting coats and $100-300 for scent proof hunting coats. Expect to pay $40 - 80 for non scent proof hunting pants and $80-300 for scent proof pants. You are probably better off with scent proof, but it is unnecessary if your other scent control measures (covered later) are in good shape.

In the cold many people like having a skin tight, sweat absorbing base layer. Long underwear is not the same as a base layer. Long underwear is just another layer of clothing, whereas a skin tight sweat absorbing layer can make a lot of difference if you are moving a lot in the cold and are sweating. You will be much warmer with your sweat absorbed away.

The standard layer of clothing, in any climate, is jeans and a t-shirt. So long as they do not smell like whatever you were doing before hunting, jeans and a t shirt are good to wear to your hunting location and then under your other articles of clothing.

Blue jeans are not acceptable to wear as an outer layer. Blue jeans nearly glow in the dark. While hunting you want to match the darkness of the night as it gets late. The way to do that is to wear camouflage clothing that is meant to fade into black, rather than our usual clothes which are meant to be bright.

Your jeans and any medium weight camouflage pants are usually enough to keep you warm all by themselves. A base layer for your legs can help though.

Many people find that a coat and standard pants allow cold air to hit you in the lower back while sitting. Camouflage overalls do everything standard camouflage pants do and give your lower back complete coverage.

Another layer to add is a heavy sweatshirt. A hood is, without a doubt, the best way to keep your neck and ears warm. I have a brown hooded sweatshirt that I wear when it gets colder out. A black, brown, or green hooded sweatshirt will provide warmth and keep your neck and ears warm. A sweatshirt may not have been made in hunting in mind, so using a UV killer on it will be important.

Hoods are great for keeping warm, but they do limit how much you can hear. And hearing is the most common way we first detect deer. Wear the hood up only when necessary.

Hoods on coats are usually in the way and aren't necessary all that often, so having one of your additional layers have the hood is a good way to go.

A Cabela's Windshear sweater is my all-time favorite article of clothing. I've worn it and a t-shirt in very low temperatures and howling wind, and said, "is that all the cold you've got?" That may have been what I was thinking, I don't recall if I could feel my face. If you're cold while hunting, buy a heavy Windshear sweater.

For boots, three hunters I know of (including me) have thrown rubber knee boots away in the past year because of how cold and uncomfortable they are to wear. But I have just discovered Irish Setter boots which are excellent so far, except they squeak when rubbed against a treestand. The advantage of rubber boots is to minimize smells.

Instead of, or in addition to, your rubber boots you will want light and brown hiking boots, and heavy cold weather boots. My last pair of hiking boots were made by (make that "marketed by") Columbia, and I am indifferent to how well they've performed. (Four years 'til they fell apart, literally.) My new Keen boots lasted 20 days before literally falling apart. I hear good things about Danner boots though, and I just bought a $315 pair of Danners.

You may also want another pair of boots to do food plot or other work in; that sweat and those smells should not be on your hunting clothing.

You want your light boots to fit comfortably in standard socks, and your heavy boots to be roomy. The air that is in your boots with your feet is an extra insulating layer.

Wool socks are the only way to go in the cold. And toe warmers that stick to your socks can be downright essential when its really cold. Standard socks plus wool socks and toe warmers in good boots is the warmest you can keep your feet out in the cold.

Next you'll need gloves. I usually keep only a light glove on my right hand, and it in a pocket when its cold, and I'll wear layers of gloves as heavy as is needed on my left hand which is invariably holding my bow or rifle. Leave spare pairs of gloves in your truck, because you'll lose them often. Cheap jersey gloves cost around $12 and are fine on their own or as a layer for most of the year.

As with every other area, layering your gloves is much warmer than only having one layer of clothing.

Also, you'll need a hat. I prefer a hooded sweatshirt to a hat with flaps or whatever. No matter how large those flaps are it is impossible to get your whole neck covered by a hat and a coat collar. A hood is very clearly the way to go.

Some hunters advocate avoiding large billed hats because when we turn our heads the large bill is more noticeably moving. Otherwise any hat, camouflage, brown, or whatever, is fine.

Lastly you'll need a face mask, or face paint. Get one that's made of cloth and quiet, or it may contribute to you missing a 170+ B&C buck. (Stupid face mask.)

If any article of your hunting clothing causes you to lose a deer, because it made noise, or whatever, get rid of it, it is worse than useless. I once had six bucks come in to me, in single file, and when I leaned away from the tree to shoot the biggest one, my new camouflage coat sounded like Velcro leaving the bark.

Obviously the bucks heard it and escaped. Guess how often I've worn that coat since.

I'm not sure that all "hunting" products were designed or tested by people who actually hunt. If you find something you like, buy two right away, it'll probably be discontinued before you look to replace your wore out one.

22

Choosing Your Weapons

The most efficient tool to shoot deer with is a rifle. Shotguns, muzzleloaders, handguns, bows and crossbows can also be used, but the most efficient weapon is a rifle.

The laws where you hunt will determine what type of firearm that you may use. Some places, notably in Alberta, do not allow any firearm to be used for hunting deer. Some places allow firearms for the length of their deer seasons, and some places have an archery season, a muzzleloader season, and a firearm season. (Who says we live in a free country?)

The reason the use of firearms is limited, I'm told, is for safety. Some places do not like guns of any sort. And some places think that handguns, muzzleloaders, and shotguns are preferable to rifles because rifle bullets travel farther than the projectiles from the other gun types.

For the most part you'll be legally required to hunt with whatever the law says for that particular time.

For cleaning your rifle you will need something like "Rem Oil" which can comes in an aerosol can. You will also need cleaning patches that are of the similar size of your gun, clean "rags" to wipe the outside of your gun in oil, and a cleaning rod that fits in your rifle.

In order to clean you should first make sure to dry your gun whenever it gets wet, use a clean rag to wipe all of the metal gun parts down with the rem oil, and put some oil on the patches and put them through the hole at the end of the cleaning rod, and then push the rod through the gun barrel, replace the patch after each push through, and repeat as necessary.

Each type of weapon is covered in the following chapters.

23

Rifles

The basics of a rifle include the barrel, which is the metal tube through which the bullets go through. A rifle is so named because the barrel of a rifle has ridges that spin around the inside of it. This is known as rifling. The rifling makes the bullet spin and therefore makes the gun more accurate than it would be without the rifling. A football is thrown with a spiral for the same reason. The end of the barrel that is not surrounded by other gun parts is the muzzle. The back end of the barrel is known as the breech.

A gun is either a muzzleloader, in which case it is loaded from the front. Or a gun is a breach loader, in which case it is loaded from the middle.

The breech end of the barrel is also known as the chamber. The chamber is where a cartridge is located when it is fired.

The metal part of the gun, in the middle, where all of the activity takes place, is the gun's action. The different action types will be elaborated upon later in the chapter.

The wood, or plastic, part of a rifle is known as the stock. The widest part of the stock, at the back, is known as the butt. The thin part just behind the trigger is known as the grip. The farthest forward part of the stock is known as the fore grip. Some rifles have their stocks divided into two pieces and some have their stocks as one piece.

Generally you want to use a gun with a wood stock in Africa, because a plastic stock would look out of place. And when you hunt where it is very wet or cold, you will want a gun that has a plastic stock because it will hold up better. Thumb hole type gun stocks are not recommended because they are awkward to use.

Some rifles have a fore sight and a rear sight on top of the barrel. For the most part, they are not used for hunting deer nowadays. These are known as open sights, or iron sights. These days we hunt deer with telescopic sights ('scopes) instead. A scope has scope mounts and rings which are attached to the top of the action of the gun.

There are several varieties of rifle. The way one rifle variety is differentiated from another is by its action. The action of a rifle is the means by which another cartridge is made ready to fire.

Rifle actions are: fully automatic, semi automatic, pump action, bolt action, lever action, and single shot. (Double barreled rifles are too expensive for our purposes, $10,000+.) Fully automatic firearms have been illegal to own in the United States since 1934. Depending on whatever so called "assault weapon" ban that we have in place, some semi automatic firearms will also be illegal to own. (Tip: when an "assault weapon" ban is in place it is generally the black plastic stocked semi automatics that are banned; wood stocked ones will generally still be legal; because a black gun is apparently more lethal.)

I am told that most firearms enthusiasts go through a point where they (including me) think that a single shot rifle would be cool to have. You can certainly hunt deer successfully with a single shot rifle, but not having a fast second shot may cost you a deer. If you do not currently want to own a single shot rifle, then let me direct your attention to the Ruger No. 1 (ruger.com). I don't recommend hunting deer with one though.

Fully automatic rifles have been banned, some semi automatics may, or may not, be banned, and single shot rifles are not your best choice of action for hunting deer. This leaves us with some semi automatic rifles, pump action rifles, bolt action rifles, and lever action rifles as our best choices for hunting whitetail deer.

Many thousands of whitetail deer are shot with each rifle action every year. And your favorite deer gun may be a gun with any one of those actions.

Sporting rifles have generally followed the technology of the military's weapons. Since the adoption of the Mauser '98 rifle as the German armed forces' official small arm (in 1898) the bolt-action rifle has been the standard big game hunting weapon.

A bolt-action rifle has many advantages over its predecessor, the lever action rifle. One important advantage is the fact that you can operate a bolt action without removing your eye from your target. Another advantage is that a bolt-action allows you to use conical (pointed) bullets. In a lever rifle the cartridges are stored end to end. And a pointed bullet would have a tendency to fire the cartridge in front of it. In a bolt rifle the cartridges are stored vertically, and therefore pointed bullets can be used.

The biggest problem with lever action rifles is the one that will prevent me from ever deer hunting with one. The cartridges available in lever action rifles are limited to cartridges unsuitable for shooting at more than one hundred yards. Because the bullets used in lever guns are slow, heavy, and not very aerodynamic their ballistics mean that they do not fly as straight as a bullet fired from a rifle with another action. You do not want to hunt with a .30-30 or .45-70 even though many deer have been killed with them.

The way a bolt action works is: A spring loaded magazine pushes cartridges up from below the bolt. When you lift the bolt handle up then back the top cartridge in the magazine moves up in front of the bolt. Then you push the bolt forward to put the cartridge into place for a shot. Then the bolt handle is rotated down to lock the bolt into place. These steps are repeated for each shot.

One advantage that a bolt action rifle has over a semi automatic is that a bolt action is more accurate. If you plan on shooting past two or three hundred yards then this may be a significant advantage. At less than two hundred yards you probably won't be able to tell the difference in accuracy between a good bolt and a good semi auto.

Another advantage is the simplicity of a bolt action. The fewer moving parts should make it more reliable, although you may not notice the difference so long as you maintain your gun well.

Eventually the U.S. military switched to a semi-automatic rifle as its standard small arm. Due to the "assault weapon" ban in the '90's many styles of semi automatics were banned from the public. Since that stupid law has expired there has been a rise in hunters using semi automatics.

There are two main shapes of semi automatic rifles. But both work the same way.

The way a semi -automatic works is a bit more complicated than bolt actions. The parts that you should know are: A magazine spring pushes cartridges up against the bottom of the bolt (same as a bolt action). Instead of a large handle, there is a small tab, or similar, that you pull back as far as possible and this allows the top cartridge to rise in front of the bolt. Then you let the bolt go and it slams forward and the cartridge is pushed into place in front of it.

Then when you pull the trigger the recoil of the shot pushes the bolt backwards. During this after shot motion the fired (spent) cartridge is ejected out of the side and the next one rises into place in front of the bolt. Then a spring moves the bolt and the cartridge in front of it forward and back into place. This process (from trigger pull to bolt movement back to bolt movement forward) is repeated each time that you pull the trigger, until the magazine is empty.

A semi automatic rifle requires a trigger pull for each shot, while a fully automatic rifle can shoot multiple times with one sustained trigger pull. Many people, especially those who want to ban guns, can never seem to understand this fact.

The big advantage that a semi automatic has over a bolt action is the speed with which you can fire your next shot. For the most part, while deer hunting, this will not matter because you should only use one shot per deer. But having a, slightly quicker, second shot at the ready can be useful and it is comforting to have in the back of your mind.

A disadvantage of hunting with a semi automatic is that you need to let the bolt slam forward after each time the magazine is filled. This is loud and may scare deer. This noise factor can be even more critical towards the end of gun season when we sometimes move in a bit closer to known bedding areas. My dad lost a chance at a nice buck once because he tried to slow the slamming of the bolt, in an attempt to be quieter, and it did not correctly seat the cartridge, and it did not fire.

A non-hunting advantage to a semi auto is if the country descends into chaos once we finally go bankrupt, then it would be a good idea to defend yourself with a gun with more firepower than a bolt action provides. A bolt action is what you want if you are going to sneak up on your target and only use one shot. A semi auto or illegal fully automatic weapon is what you want if you need to defend yourself against multiple targets.

There are all sorts of bolt action rifles and semi auto rifles that you can get. And after deciding on your desired action, the next step is to pick out a gun model. This will often be determined by your preferences and budget.

Features such as magazine size, stock materiel, and so on will not affect your deer hunting too much. All a rifle needs to do is put one shot, or two, on target.

Winchester, Remington, Ruger, Browning, Kimber, Savage, Tikka, Sako, CZ and others all make fine rifles. Look at their websites, find a gun dealer and have a look at a lot of them.

And since everyone who reads books like this wants specific recommendations, I'll say that a fine deer hunting rifle to get is a Winchester Model 70. There are many varieties of Model 70s and all are fine. Stick a Vortex Viper riflescope on top and you'll be set.

A less expensive, and yet still acceptable, option would be a Ruger American Rifle and a Vortex Diamondback 'scope.

Once you've selected your preferred make and model, you'll want to look at the list of cartridges available for that particular rifle.

24

Cartridges

Before we look at which bullet, or slug, that you should use, it is important to understand how a projectile is sent downrange.

A cartridge, or shotgun shell, is a contained charge of gunpowder, bullet, and firing primer.

The bullet is the pointy, flat, or rounded part which is half hidden by the brass case. Inside the case there is an amount of gunpowder. Opposite of the bullet there is a primer. Centerfire cartridges have the primer visible as the circle inside the flat end of the cartridge. Rimfire cartridges will not have the smaller circle inside of the flat end of the cartridge. The brass case holds the whole thing together.

Rimfire cartridges are used by only very small cartridges. Cartridges used to hunt deer are all centerfire. You can kill deer with rimfire rifles, but I am not recommending it, and it may not be legal to do so where you hunt anyway.

A shotgun cartridge is the same thing except instead of a bullet you will have "shot" (not often used for hunting deer anymore) or a "slug" in a plastic cylinder rather than a brass one.

Basically, what a gun is a tube (the barrel), a handle (the stock), a means of putting another cartridge into place to be fired (the action), a trigger to fire the gun, and the firing pin which strikes the primer and sets off the cartridge.

The firing pin of a gun is a metal pin that, when the trigger is pulled, strikes the primer. The primer sparks and ignites the gunpowder. Because burning gunpowder creates heat the gases contained behind the bullet, or slug, expand. The expanding gases need someplace to escape through. Because of the way a cartridge is built the easiest way for the heated gases to escape is to push the projectile out of the cartridge. Only friction holds the cartridge in place. The projectile is pushed, by the heated gas down the barrel and then downrange.

The projectile will spin through the barrel thanks to the rifling in the barrel. And a shotgun slug will not spin, unless it is a rifled slug or is shot from a rifled slug gun.

An interesting physics fact is that a bullet dropped from and one fired from the same height will both land on the ground at the same time. The dropped bullet will land at your feet, and the fired bullet will land a long ways away, but at the same time. I can't imagine how this could be tested in practice.

One more thing to note is a sabot, which you may find in a shotgun or muzzleloader. A sabot is fitted around the projectile so that only the sabot, and not the projectile touch the barrel. The sabot will fall away from the projectile as soon as they leave the barrel and the projectile will continue to the target.

Rifle cartridges come in infinite sizes. Pick a number between .17 and .600 (that's 0.17 and 0.6 inches.) and you can, just about, have a rifle with a cartridge that size.

However, cartridges like .17 HMR, .22 Long Rifle, and .223 are what you would use to hunt squirrels, rabbits, and coyotes. On the other end of the size range, cartridges like .416 Rigby, .450 Nitro Express, and .450/500 are used to hunt dangerous game like lions, tigers, and elephants.

For hunting whitetail deer you'll want a rifle cartridge in the range of .257 Roberts at the small end to .300 Win Mag at the big end. A .300 Wing Mag is probably better suited to moose, but I've killed bucks with that cartridge. This range also includes cartridges measured metrically too. 6mm is a bit small but 6.5mm and 7mm rifles are good for whitetail deer.

Incidentally, you can multiply the metric size by four to compare its size to imperially measured cartridges. For example, a 7mm is .284 inches in diameter, and you could hunt with a .280 Win which is .284 inches in diameter. You cannot interchange bullets, but you can multiply by four to compare sizes.

One more "interesting" fact about bullets is that their name is not necessarily reflective of their actual diameter. For example a .270 bullet is actually more like .277 inches in diameter. A .280

Rem is actually .284, and .308 Win, .30-06 Sprng, .30-30, .300 Win Mag, and others all have a diameter of .308 inches. You cannot interchange these cartridges, but the bullets, as opposed to the cartridges, are all the same diameter.

Note that the size of a bullet is only the size of the projectile. The size of the case will differ with the amount of gunpowder contained.

Remember that the "bullet" is the projectile that is fired downrange and the "cartridge" consists of a bullet, case, primer, and powder.

Also note that the British measure their cartridges differently than Americans do. (They're weird.) Unless you buy a rifle from an English make, or have a .303, you'll not need to think about it, but it is a fact nonetheless.

A Texas deer hunter may rightfully claim that a .243 Win is ideal for whitetail deer. And an Ontario deer hunter may rightfully claim that a .30-06 is better. This difference of opinion comes from the different sizes of deer and the differences in hunting conditions.

Hunting in thick brush should point you towards a slow, heavy, blunt bullet like a .30-30 (that's the theory, don't actually hunt with a .30-30). And hunters who expect to kill a deer at 300 yards will want something more like a .270 Win.

There are all sorts of other arguments to be made about what cartridge is best for which situation. There are lots of personal preferences and lots of cartridges available. But there is no cartridge that is best for every situation. I have shot deer with a number of cartridges including: .257 Roberts, 7x57 Mauser, 2.70 Winchester, .308 Winchester, .30-06 Springfield, and .300 Winchester Magnum. My experience would be is that a bullet in the heart or lungs results in a dead deer.

My longest shot at a whitetail was 138 B&C thirteen pointer that I shot offhand at 189 yards with the .257 Roberts. My shortest shot on a buck was at 5 yards from a ground blind with a .300 Winchester Magnum. Any cartridge from the .257 Roberts up to the .300 Winchester Magnum is perfectly acceptable for most whitetail hunting.

Rather than go through the merits of lots of rifle cartridges, I'm going to point you to three. These three cartridges are widely available, accurate, time tested, and have killed thousands of deer each. I've also killed a buck, or more, with each. With any one of these you should be in good shape to shoot bucks at ten yards or three hundred and ten yards. If you want to shoot elk or coyotes too, then these cartridges will do nicely in those tasks as well.

.270 Winchester, .308 Winchester, and .30-06 Springfield are three good whitetail cartridges. You can buy a rifle with any of these cartridges and be set for life.

Don't forgo your selected rifle if one of these cartridges is not an option; remember that bullet sizes from .257 to .308 are fine for deer. The three cartridges I have selected are merely those which will cover every possibility well and you should have no trouble finding another box of cartridges at any appropriate store.

Pick your action, pick your make and model, and then pick one of that gun's available cartridges; .270, .308, and .30-06 preferred.

Once you become more advanced as a hunter you will want to buy guns with different cartridges, and you may even load your own cartridges.

Now that we've narrowed your cartridge selection down we need to decide on which type of that particular cartridge you want to use.

For each caliber there are numerous different options. One differentiation is the bullet weight, measured in grains. ("Grains" being a unit of measurement like pounds or grams.) The lighter the bullet the faster it will go. If there is too much gunpowder for the bullet, it will not be as controlled and accurate. On the other end of the range, a heavy bullet with little powder behind it will produce a very slow moving bullet. Bullets designed for deer will likely be between 90 grains (very small) and 200 grains (a bit big).

Heavier bullets will hit harder and lighter bullets will go faster, and therefore farther.

After the bullet weight you can decide on the bullet itself. There are all sorts of bullet designs for all sorts of purposes. Some bullets have "full metal jackets" and will retain their shape after hitting the target. On the other end some bullets will have hollow points that expand the bullet into a bigger shape when it hits the target; pointy and aerodynamic when flying and as big as possible once the target is hit.

The expanding of the bullet occurs with either a hollow point or some materiel other than the copper bullet case (as opposed to the brass cartridge case) is at the tip of the bullet. When the target is struck the bullet will expand when the tip is moved backwards through the bullet and the copper case "mushrooms" into a bigger shape. This bigger shape will do more damage.

The small fast expanding bullets will often explode on impact, which is good for rodents. (You may want to YouTube: "exploding groundhogs" or "exploding prairie dogs".) But an expanding bullet may only do superficial damage to large heavy boned animals like buffalo. As far as bullet makers are concerned, whitetail deer are light, thin skinned animals, for which you want an expanding bullet that doesn't expand so fast that it explodes. You want the bullet to mushroom but stay together to pass right through the deer.

You won't really need to worry about any of that so long as you get a good name brand cartridges. Ammunition manufacturers like: Barnes, Federal, Hornady, and Winchester are all good. Each gun will shoot a bit differently in each gun, so you will want to try several different cartridges to see which you like the best. Once you find what you like, stick with that and only use that specific cartridge.

In order to find out what your gun likes best you can get a piece of paper and see how small the group is at, say, 100 yards. A "group" will be five shots from the same place and same distance, with the diameter of the smallest circle in which each of the five shots hits as the group's diameter. A diameter of one inch is better than two inches because each shot is closer to hitting the same place each time.

And then when you find one you like...stick with it.

25

Buying a Gun

Browning, Remmington, Winchester, Ruger, Kimber, Sako, and many other companies all make fine rifles.

And we've narrowed your list of actions down to semi-automatic and bolt actions.

We've also limited your cartridge selection to between .257 and .308.

So go to one of the above mentioned companies and pick out a bolt or semi-automatic with an appropriate cartridge.

A good new rifle may cost from four hundred dollars (Ruger American Rifle) and up to as much as you like.

If you don't have several hundred to spend, then you're looking at a used gun. Go to a store like Cabela's which sells used guns and pick out one with the above recommendations. You could go to a gun show, but private sellers are more likely to sell you a gun with issues. If you don't know, go to a trusted gun dealer that deals with used guns. Avoid rust and any guns with aspects you question. When the buck arrives you want to think about shooting him, not worrying about your gun.

Gun sights are an important aspect of your rifle. Telescopic sights gather more light and allow you to shoot better in low light, than do open or, "iron," sights. They also make long distance shots easier. Many guys say they'd rather have the best 'scope and only an okay gun, rather than the other way around. 'scopes are important.

An okay gun is nearly as good as an excellent one for most deer hunting. And the best optics are massively better for all shooting done during dawn and dusk, when the deer are most active.

So you need a 'scope. Acceptable options include 'scopes from brands like: Leupold, Zeiss, Swarovski, Nikon, Vortex, and the Cabela's Euro is good too. Get the most expensive 'scope you can afford. You'll want either a fixed power like 4X, or something like a variable 3-9X. (That's four times magnification, and from three to nine times magnification, etc.) A 'scope's statistics will list its "objective lens" diameter. 42mm is the standard size, don't go smaller; bigger is okay.

Although its easy enough to mount a 'scope yourself, its probably best if you let a professional mount it for you. And he can deal with matching the 'scope rings to the 'scope and the gun.

Swarovski 'scopes are about as good as it gets. My Swarovski seems to give me about fifteen more minutes at dusk and dawn than any other riflescope. But they cost an awful lot. Buy the best 'scope that you can.

My specific recommendation is that you should get anything that says "Swarovski" on it. They are clearly the best.

If you're not made of money, then get the most expensive Vortex riflescope that you can. I have spent some time selling bows and optics at a sporting goods store and I have never, ever, ever heard anything bad ever about anything from Vortex, ever. Your riflescope options will start at a bit under $200. Get the most expensive 'scope that you can though.

You aren't expected to have every single detail about your gun memorized, but you will alert others to your novice ability if you do not at least know the name of your rifle, your 'scope's name and cartridge; for example: a .30-06 Winchester Model 70 with a Vortex Viper."

26

Gun Safety

Gun safety can be a big problem for some people, and you'll likely be obligated to go through a hunter's safety class prior to being allowed to buy a hunting license. In the interest of being thorough, I'll go through most of the gun safety points you should know.

Don't point any gun at anything you don't want shot, and likely dead. This means unloaded guns too.

Leave your safety on at all times, but don't rely on it for your protection.

Don't put anything in the trigger guard unless you plan on shooting something. As in, keep your finger out of the trigger guard unless you are about to shoot something. And keep the trigger guard free of obstructions.

Don't pull your gun up to your tree when there are cartridges in it.

Always use the correct cartridge for your gun. If your gun says ".308 Win" on the barrel, then you should only ever use cartridges that say ".308 Win" on them.

Keep kids and any who you don't trust away from the guns.

Don't shoot a gun if you are concerned about its safety, avoid rust, etc.

Keep the barrel clear of obstruction. Some dirt in your barrel could prevent the projectile from leaving the gun and cause the barrel to explode.

Know what is behind your target. Don't shoot towards where there are people.

Don't use your 'scope to look at things that might be people.

Beware of double loading your muzzleloader, because anything that explodes when you hold it is not good.

Have some sort of plan for when your government tries to confiscate them.

27

Shooting a Gun

I'd like to point out that I am by no means an expert shot, and that this chapter is meant to explain the basics of shooting for those of you who are unfamiliar with shooting. For more advanced shooting recommendations, you'll need to look elsewhere.

Don't go to your hunting property and shoot your gun a day, or so, before the season because it may scare the deer. You should be shooting and practicing all summer long and avoid unnecessary shooting near the deer you are going to hunt near the time you will be hunting them.

In the interest of avoiding being sued for not recommending it: a gun is very loud and hearing and eye protection should be worn.

I am going to say that there are three types of gun shooting as it relates to hunting: sighting-in, practicing, and taking a shot at an animal.

The range at which you shoot will be determined by the space you have and the gun you have. You might sight a pistol, shotgun, or old muzzleloader in at 25 or 50 yards and a rifle or modern muzzleloader at 100 yards.

Shooting a rifle or muzzleloader is different from shooting a shotgun. When shooting a shotgun you will pull the trigger. When shooting a rifle or muzzleloader you need to squeeze the trigger. That's squeeeeeeze the trigger. Pulling the trigger of rifle the same as you pull a shotgun trigger may move the gun a bit and throw the bullet off target. Squeeeeeze the trigger in a way that almost surprises you with when the gun is specifically fired. You may unconsciously brace yourself for the recoil if you know, specifically, when to expect it.

Gravity makes more of an impact on your shooting the longer your shooting is done at. Because a bullet will hit earth eventually accurate shooting requires taking the rate of fall of the bullet into account.

Faster, more powerful, cartridges, like the .270 Win, .308 Win, and .30-06 Sprg. that I recommend to you beginning hunters, and everyone else, each has their own unique rate of drop that will be around three inches at three hundred yards. The way rifles that fire these cartridges are generally sighted in is by having them dead center right to left and three inches high at 100 yards. Sighting-in this way will result in the bullet hitting three inches high at 100 yards, approximately "on" at 200 yards, and three inches low at 300 yards. This means that you can aim right where you want your bullet to hit the deer anywhere between 10 yards and 300 yards away and never be more than three inches off from where you aim.

There are those that criticize this way of sighting your rifle in, and you should change to fit certain circumstances like 500 yard shots, etc., but this is the standard that you should first use when shooting high powered cartridges like the three that I recommend.

If you plan to hunt with some other cartridge, or a shotgun, muzzleloader, or pistol, then you can go shoot and take note of the results at different ranges or you can look for sighting in recommendations elsewhere.

Sighting a gun in is the aligning the sights up with where the bullets, or slugs, hit the target. Sighting-in should be done at least once per year, but you should also be practicing throughout the year and.

Sighting in is done to make sure that you hit where you aim, because this is so, and unlike practicing you should shoot off of a rest. Shooting "off-hand" has some room for wiggle and movement. You do not stand perfectly still and so your gun will not be perfectly still when you shoot. Sighting-in should be done in a way that removes as much of the human element as possible. You want to make sure that your gun is good before you see how good you are.

Shooting off of a rest can be done by buying a shooting bench, building a shooting bench, or shooting at a shooting range which will have a bench. On top of the bench you will want to place a dedicated shooting bag or a sand bag to conform to the gun and give you as stable a rest as possible.

If you have no access to any of that you might just wad a shirt up and put it on top of a bench or your truck's hood to shoot from.

One thing that non-shooters get confused about is comparing where the bullets hit with where the "bull's-eye" is. Good shooting should result in all of the bullets hitting in the same place as each other. Ideally each bullet will go through the same hole, when fired from the same shooter, at the same range, from the same gun. In practice what you want is the smallest grouping of target hits. The standard group of shots is five. When you see the group numbers in a magazine what you are seeing is the measurement of the diameter of the circle that surrounds the five shots of the group. A shot group within a circle with a one inch diameter is much better than the shot group inside a circle with a two inch diameter. This is true even if the second group is in the center of the target and the first group is way off in some corner of the target.

A tight grouping means that you, your gun, and your cartridges are shooting consistently and accurately. A wide grouping, even if it is closer to the center of the target, says that no one knows where the next bullet will hit. (What I wouldn't give to never need to explain this paragraph ever again...)

When your grouping is small you will need to adjust your sight so that your group moves over to where your target is. The number of sights, and sight adjustments, is too vast for me to list them all. But you should take my advice and add a telescopic sight to your deer hunting gun (Swarovski or Vortex preferred).

The way to adjust a 'scope is to fire a shot, take note of where the projectile hits in relation to where your sights were on the target; two inches low and three to the right, for example. There will be two bulges in the middle of the 'scope. One will be on one side and one will be on top. They will likely, but not always, have a screw on cover. One will be the height adjuster, and the other will be the horizontal adjuster. There will be an arrow pointing clockwise, or counterclockwise and say "up," "L," or "R."

Knowing which way to adjust can take some thinking. Think about how moving the sight up means that the gun barrel, and therefore the shot, will be moved down, in order for the sight to still be on the target. Moving the sight to the left will cause the gun barrel to move to the right for the sight to stay on the target. Chase the shot; a shot low and left means you should move your sight down and to the left.

In addition to an arrow and direction your 'scope will likely say something like: "1 click = ¼ inch at 100 yards". Note that 'scopes from outside of America will use metric measurements, but they will be similar. To make the adjustment, turn the knob, or put a coin in the indent and move it the required number of clicks.

Then shoot again, check your results, and repeat as necessary.

One of history's best rifle shots, W.D.M. Bell, (you should read "Bell of Africa") was known to carry his rifle around when he was not hunting and dry fire his unloaded gun on occasion. The thinking is that you should carry your gun around until it becomes a part of you. When you shoot without a cartridge in the gun, dry fire, you shoot be quickly putting your gun to your shoulder and having your sights on your target as soon as the gun is up.

Because of the way each gun and person fit with each other where the sights are some guns will fit you better. You might try picking out a target, putting your gun up and noting how close to your target your sights are immediately.

Sighting-in should be done off of a rest but you should practice without one, to get as comfortable and confident as possible.

Stop practicing if you are tired or begin to flinch at your gun's recoil. Shooting after this point is unlikely to be productive or accurate.

The third type of shooting is when you are shooting at a deer. This will be covered in a later chapter; after we know which specific deer to shoot.

28

Muzzleloaders

Muzzleloaders can be so accurate that your shooting range will be limited by your ability and not the gun's. Old time muzzleloaders and even those from ten years ago were nowhere near as accurate as those of today. You might use a flintlock muzzleloader to look more stylish while hunting, but you would not be doing your best to shoot deer. All of the non-new muzzleloaders will also be so difficult to take apart and clean that you may skip some hunting just so that you do not have to clean your gun.

You'll want a new, or newish, CVA or Thompson Center brand muzzleloader.

You'll get it in .50 caliber because .50 caliber is the standard size for which you'll be able to buy stuff for. You may prefer a .45 caliber, but finding the appropriate stuff for it may be quite difficult and therefore not worth the bother.

Your muzzleloader will need accessories, a 'scope (just like your rifle's, but there are such things as shotgun slug gun 'scopes with various horizontal crosshairs for varying distances, and that may be ideal for you), you'll need gunpowder, for which I recommend getting the Hogden 50 grain cylindrical clumps of powder rather than going through the slow and difficult measuring of the grains, and you'll also need some sort of bullet or saboted bullet. Bullets that have the sabots attached to them will make loading your gun simpler too; look for something like a "powerbelt."You'll also need many tons of cleaning rags for your muzzleloader and you'll probably want to clean your gun between every other shot, because muzzleloaders are unbelievably dirty. If you shoot a few times before cleaning you are likely to need to spend an honest hour cleaning the gun afterwords.

Loading a muzzleloader will be done by putting the same amount of gun powder down the end of the barrel each time, then pushing the bullet, or sabot down the barrel as far down as it goes with the ramrod that comes with the gun. Then you'll want to put a primer in the back (breech) of the gun.

I use two of the fifty grain Hogden blackpowder cylinders and the powerbelt bullets that have a plastic belt that means that you do not need to bother with things like a sabot, a bullet and/ or a patch.

A ramrod that is shorter than the barrel may be hard to extract after it has packed the powder and bullet down. I recommend getting a ramrod extender to make things easier.

You will want to be exceedingly careful with muzzleloaders, I have heard of many hands lost when muzzleloaders explode. You will need to do some more research about your specific gun to learn about how it works.

29

Shotguns

Shotguns are meant for hitting small targets, flying targets, or things when you have little time, or ability, to precisely aim. Shotguns are better at hitting hard to hit targets because they can shoot multiple projectiles at once.

Where deer are concerned you do not want to use shot of any sort. You can hunt with and kill deer with buckshot, but your effective range will be short and you will leave lots of the shot in the meat, which you'll not want to eat later.

If you are only legally able to hunt deer with a shotgun during certain seasons than what you'll want to shoot with your shot gun is a "slug." A slug is a large, single piece, projectile.

For the most part, the shotgun actions are similar to rifle actions. But the actions that you'll want to use with shotguns are different. Your slug gun should be a semi-automatic, pump, or break action gun.

You cannot just shoot slugs through any shotgun. You will want to find someone who knows about the gun you are considering in order to see if it can shoot slugs. One thing that can prevent the safe firing of slugs is the "choke" of the gun.

Because shotguns generally fire "shot" there are varying ways that that shot can leave the gun. In order to vary the shot's "pattern" some shotguns have the ends of their barrels narrowed to change how the shot flies, these are varying types of chokes..

Some places legally limit the guns to can hunt deer with to shotguns. The reason for this is that the lawmakers in those places like to annoy hunters. A rifle can easily be shot accurately by you or me, assuming you have some minimal knowledge, out past two hundred yards. A shotgun slug will run out of a lot of steam at one hundred yards. This is because shotgun slugs are bigger, heavier, and slower than bullets.

Like anything else, you should practice with your shotgun at twenty, fifty, and one hundred yards, at least, in order to understand how the slugs fly. (Hint: heavy slugs are more affected by gravity.)

Browning, Mossberg, Remington, and Winchester all make fine shotguns. Buy a dedicated "slug gun" to hunt deer with.

As far as we're concerned, there are two sizes of shotguns: twelve gauge and twenty gauge. A shotgun's gauge is similar to a rifle's caliber in that they are both the measurement of size.

If you are a young boy, or a woman, you will be better off shooting the smaller twenty gauge shotguns. They are less powerful and so they have less "kick," or "recoil," than the bigger twelve gauges do. Shooting a gun that is too big for you can cause you to become scared of the gun's recoil, which will cause your shooting to be inaccurate.

Don't use too big of a gun.

For the rest of you, twelve gauge shotguns are bigger, more powerful, and you'll have more options with them.

Talk to somebody at wherever you plan on buying your slugs to get the best ones for you. Whatever is most popular is fine, but don't buy anything just because some guy on TV was paid to tell you that it is good.

As with everything else, practice as much as possible with only one kind, and size, of slug at varying distances until you understand where the slugs hit at those different ranges.

30

Bows

In some states, and provinces, there are archery specific deer hunting seasons. During these seasons you are only allowed to hunt deer with some sort of bow. So, you'll need to get one to maximize your time in the woods.

For those of you who don't know, a bow is a weapon with two limbs that bend when you pull on the string that connects them, and when the string is released the limbs straighten the string propels the arrow, or bolt, downrange. A bowstring does not stretch, much.

Shooting a deer with a bow is much more difficult than shooting a deer with a firearm. Much more skill is needed to shoot a bow accurately and a bow's effective range is quite short. Do not expect to shoot deer with your bow past fifty yards, unless you practice at much further ranges an awful lot. Shots past thirty yards are not always easy either. On your first year of deer hunting you may not want to take shots at deer at more than twenty yards.

Once you've decided that you want to take advantage of your local archery season, you'll need to buy a bow and some bow accessories.

There are three types of bows with which you might hunt deer: traditional bows (longbows and recurves), compound bows, and crossbows.

Let me rephrase that: if you want to successfully hunt deer during archery season, you'll need to buy a compound bow or a crossbow. Traditional bows are much more stylish, and it is more of an accomplishment to kill a deer with a traditional bow, because it is immeasurably more difficult. I'll be impressed if you shoot a buck with a traditional bow, but I'm not recommending it.

The amount of practice necessary to shoot a traditional bow well is a lot, as in if you plan to hunt with a traditional bow you need to be shooting it daily for many months in advance. The biggest problem with traditional bows is that your extreme shooting range with one is something like thirty yards, if that.

So if you want to bow hunt deer as stylishly as possible buy a longbow or recurve. Bear and Martin make good traditional bows, but if you are serious about hunting with one you should consider having one custom made for you. You will also want to shoot fixed, not mechanical, broadheads in the Bear Razorhead style, on arrows with feathers, not vanes, and shoot with a tab or glove of some sort, not a release.

If I sound down on traditional bows, it's only because of how much less effective they are. They do indeed look much cooler than compound bows, and their simplicity is desirable. I hunted with a recurve bow one season because I very much liked the idea of a bow with minimal parts. A traditional bow really only has four parts and if something goes wrong it will almost certainly be something wrong with your shooting and not the bow's fault.

Incidentally, I missed one buck that season, and had another arrow deflected by a branch that I did not see before I shot.

If you plan to hunt with a traditional bow, I applaud your dedication, and appreciate that you'll allow more deer to live so that I may shoot them.

Although I am giving consideration to the merits of me hunting with traditional archery.

The rest of you will want to find yourself a bow with "training wheels."

Laws will, once again, make a substantial part of your decision for you. The laws about hunting with crossbows are different for each state and change every year. In Wisconsin, as I write this, the laws are constantly changing for the ability to hunt with crossbows.

A crossbow is much more like a rifle than a bow in some ways. Once the 'scope is on and sighted in, you'll pick up the crossbow and shoot it like a rifle. You can then pass it to your friend and he will also be able to shoot it well. Compound bows are more personalized.

A crossbow has a stock, like a gun, and a horizontal, not vertical, pair of limbs, with the string behind. Most of them require something like 160 pounds to 290 pounds of force to pull the string back. This is easier than it sounds because one of your feet will be in the "stirrup," and your weight will help you. You may also add pulleys or a crank to reduce the amount of weight needed to pull the string back.

Have whoever sells you the bow show you how your specific one works. They are all reasonably simple to do, but each bow has its differences from the others.

TenPoint and Excalibur are the companies that makes the best hunting crossbows. TenPoint's lower price point brand, Wicked Ridge, is of similar quality but slower and devoid of many bells and whistles. A Wicked Ridge crossbow will start at around $450 and the best TenPoint will cost around $2000, with Excaliburs will range in similar prices. Those prices will include the bow, 'scope, quiver, and a few bolts. (Crossbows shoot "bolts," generally twenty inches long, and other bows shoot "arrows.")

If you are looking into hunting with a crossbow, do some research into which features you want at the price you are interested in, and decide accordingly, but decide on a TenPoint or Excalibur. Notice that these two brands have parts made form metal and other brands have parts made from plastic. Guess which is more likely to break.

The crossbow accessories you'll need are, a few more bolts (which will be specific to your brand of crossbow), broadheads, a crossbow specific target, and a case.

Crossbows have their place, and more states are allowing their use every year, but most of you bow hunters will use a compound bow to shoot deer.

Compound bows will be the subject of their own chapter.

31

Compound Bows

You can save some money by buying a used bow, but a bow or crossbow is not the place you want to save money. All sorts of things can go wrong with bows, and the newer bows get much better each year. You'll be doing yourself a great disservice if you do not buy yourself a new bow every few years.

Do not buy a used bow. Nothing good can come of it, and a cheap ($400 for a package deal) new bow will be, almost without exception be much better than any used bow you may get. And your used bow will probably require new cables and strings which will cost more than $100.

I'm not kidding. I've worked in a bow shop and seen the "great deals" some guys have gotten on "great bows." Don't do it. Never buy a used bow; you can buy a used gun, but not a bow.

Buy the cheapest new compound at a reputable dealer if you have limited money. And there are very likely going to be several other serious to annoying problems with them. Some of those problems may be unfixable and will prevent you from shooting the bow at all.

I'm not sure if I've ever seen a newly acquired used bow for which I'd be willing to pay $20 for.

The parts of a compound bow are: the grip, the riser, the cables, the string, the bottom cam, the top cam or idler wheel, the limbs, the arrow shelf, and the cable rod. Other parts of a compound bow that you may or may not have include: a nock, a D-loop, a peep sight, string "leeches", a sting stopper, and limb dampeners.

For the most part, you do not need to know what any of those parts are. If you buy a new bow it will have all, or most of the above mentioned parts.

The important things to know about your bow are: that you get the right handed version (or left), and that all of the parts that are on it are in good condition. If the bow is new, then all the parts should look new and not frayed or worn.

I will go over the parts you need to interact with in the next chapter, but first we need to buy a bow, and then buy some accessories.

There are a wide variety of compound bow manufacturers. Companies like Bear, Diamond, Hoyt, Matthews, Elite, Strother, and PSE all make fine bows. You might buy a bare bow or a bow package which will have most of the bow accessories that you'll need. The price range you'll be looking at will be between $400 for the least expensive package that you'd want to have, up to $1600 for the top of the line bare Hoyt.

As the price of a compound bow increases the speed the arrows fly will increase, the quality of the materials will increase, and the weight of the bow will decrease.

Picking your bow will first consist of picking your price point; second will be deciding on a brand, if you have a preference. Those two points will narrow your selection considerably. Do some research before going to your bow shop, and have one, or three, specific bow models in mind before you go.

New bows should all be perfectly fine, and much of the choice will be about price and brand preference. All the arrow speeds and bow weights will be comparable at their comparable price points.

One other point to keep in mind is that everyone's arms are of different lengths and so we all draw bows back different lengths. Many people looking for bows seem oddly fixated on what their draw length is. It is important to have your bow set to the correct draw length for you, but it is just a number. If you are a man of average height, more or less, then almost every adult bow can be made to fit you. If you are much shorter or taller than average then your bow options may be limited.

The "draw weight" is the amount of power needed to pull a bow back. Most bows have a range of ten pounds for adjustment. Most adult bow models top out at 60 or 70 pounds. More draw weight allows you to shoot further and hit harder, but if you can't pull it back, then it won't matter what the number is. Unless you are exceptionally strong, the only way to build up bow drawing muscles is to pull on a bow.

When you shoot you want it to be very easy to pull your bow back. If you need to twist around a tree to shoot, then a difficult draw will not work. Many people try to use too high of a draw weight, and struggle when the deer arrives. Use a draw weight that is comfortable.

Your bow dealer should be able to set a new bow up for your draw length and draw weight.

So, let's say you've narrowed your selection to a few models, and are at your bow shop. Pick up all of your options and see if you like the feel of the grip. (Smaller grips will shoot more accurately than larger grips.

Take your few bows to your shop's shooting range and shoot each a few times. Don't worry about hitting anything until you've picked the specific bow you want. If one feels very awkward or vibrates a lot, ask the bow shop guy to see of anything is amiss on the bow.

Notice things like how smooth the bow is to draw, and if once the bow is drawn back how much you can move forward before the bow wants to jerk you forward.

After shooting a few arrows, pick your bow. And we will move on to bow accessories.

32
Bow Accessories

If you've read every word in this book so far you will have noticed that I've outlined things to look for in clothing, treestands, rifles, and bows, and while I've made some suggestions, the specifics of these things don't matter a whole lot (so long as you're happy with them). But if there is one point I'd like to say where the specifics matter then it will be the point that follows.

After shooting a few shots with your selected bow, take note of the rest it has on it, if it is a bow package. If it does not already have a Trophy Ridge Whisker Biscuit on it you will walk over to the arrow rest section of your bow shop and pull the least expensive Whisker Biscuit, or the Whisker Biscuit "Quick Shot", or Whisker Biscuit "Kill Shot" arrow rest off the shelf. Then turn to the bow shop guy and say, "I'm buying this bow. Put this rest on for me, please."

He may say, "This package comes with this other rest. You'll need to buy it and then buy this Whisker Biscuit additionally."

And you'll reply, "I don't care. Put this rest on please."

The purpose of an arrow rest is to hold the arrow as it is drawn back and to guide it on its path downrange. The types of arrow rests on the market, for compound bows, today consists of rests that "contain" the arrow in one place and "drop away" rests. Drop away rests are touted as being more accurate. However drop away rests add more parts and more movement; and more moving parts means more things to go wrong. Things that go wrong will cost you deer.

If you want to shoot at more than, say, 50 yards or are going to competitively shoot then a drop-away arrow rest is a good idea, but for hunting deer at less than 50 yards use a Trophy Ridge Whisker Biscuit.

Back when I was shooting "fingers," rather than a release, I once drew my bow back on a buck only to have the arrow hop off the rest. When I eased my bow down and redrew with the arrow in place, the buck noticed me and ran away. I then put the original Whisker Biscuit on my bow and I have never had that problem again. (135 B&C)

Many of the bow accessories will be things that you try anew every so often. If they improve your ability to kill deer you'll keep them. If they cause you to lose opportunities at deer, get rid of them or improve them.

Nearly all of the accessories that I'm about to mention are the things that I like because I once had something else and that something else caused me to lose an opportunity at a buck. Eliminating those faulty pieces of equipment, and improving them as the technology improves is the name of the game.

A Whisker Biscuit is a metal disc, or ¾ of a disc, with brown and black bristles pointing towards the center. Your arrow will be pushed in from the ¼ of the missing disc and into the hole in the center. And one of the biggest advantages of this rest is that that arrow will be ready to shoot no matter how much you move your bow around prior to the shot. Your bow will be jostled a bit during your hunt between the time you place your arrow on your rest and the time to move to shoot.

Use a Whisker Biscuit for deer hunting, use no other arrow rest, for hunting. When you do, I will have essentially "given" you one deer you would not have gotten otherwise, because a more complex rest may go amiss.

Although I will point out that this is my book written the way I want, and other archers can make good arguments for using a "drop-away" rest. But drop-away rests have moving parts, and moving parts go wrong, and moving parts break. Hunting isn't the same as target shooting. We would do things differently for target shooting only.

Now back to general guidelines for picking hunting products.

The arrow rest is one accessory, the others that you'll need are: a front sight, a peep sight, a nock, a quiver, arrows, a target to practice at, practice (field) points, broadheads, and a release.

The front sight will be made of metal or plastic and have fiber optics which end on the end of pins. The way it will work is that you will put the glowing pin on the target that you want to hit.

There are a variety of sights at a variety of prices. Because deer are inclined to be in a position to be shot in low light conditions you'll want the brightest possible sight pins. This makes the brightness of the pins the most important aspect of a sight (assuming it is of sufficient quality to stay in place and not move around). There are two ways for a sight to be bright: a long length of fiber optics (colored plastic "wires") leading to the sight pin, or an artificial light. I prefer things to be simple, because less can go wrong, so I prefer sights with lots of fiber optics. When you look at all the sights in a store you will notice which ones have a few inches of fiber optics, and you will notice that some have fiber optics that are wrapped around part of the sight several times. You want the wrapped fiber optics or a lighted sight.

Other things to consider in a sight are the number of pins and the direction of the pins. For the most part sights come with one, three, or five pins. For example, my sight has three pins, so I use the top pin on targets twenty yards away, the second pin at thirty yards, and the bottom pin at forty yards. More pins would seem to be better, and if you plan to hunt at ranges from twenty to sixty yards they may well be. But more pins clutter up your sight and leave less room for the wrapped fiber optics for each sight. The advantage of a single sight pin is that you will practice at varying distances and become better at judging those distances. With my three pin sight I need to hold my forty yard pin above the target when I want to shoot at fifty yards, and a single pin hunter does it for nearly all distances and therefore gets more practice at it.

There are moving single pin sights, but they require additional steps between deciding to shoot and shooting, during which time more can go wrong. And moving parts are more likely to break. More likely to break means you'll shoot fewer deer. And your order of operations will be: see a deer, decide to shoot, say: "hey deer, don't move while I adjust my sight to the proper distance..."

The direction of the pins will be how they're attached to the sight, either from the bottom or the side. This is a matter of personal preference. The sights from the bottom do all line up so the pins cover up less of your target. For whatever reason I prefer pins from the side, but if you are new to shooting a bow, I'd suggest getting a sight with three pins that are attached at the bottom. You may as well start out the most logical way and not accumulate inferior preferences...not that it matters much in this case.

A final comment on sights before we move to the next accessory is that sight pins come in different colors. Usually the top pin is green, the second is yellow, and the third is red. The difference in color is meant to differentiate one pin from another, so that you are less likely to put the wrong pin on the target. Noticing that green pins are brightest in low light is something that many people fail to ever notice. While you're hunting you should be noticing things, including your equipment. There's always room for improvement. (If you don't have all the numbers printed on your bow and gun memorized by the end of the hunting season, then you haven't hunted enough or haven't noticed enough.)

Everyone's eyes are different but the way it works for me is in the evening as it grows darker, the bottom red pin disappears from sight about the time I can no longer see deer forty yards away. Then the yellow pin disappears when I can no longer see deer thirty yards away. And lastly the green pin will stay brightest longest, until it is too late to see deer anymore.

I like the Trophy Ridge and Montana Blackgold bow sights best.

That's the front sight. The back sight is called a "peep sight." A peep sight is a plastic, or metal, ring that you look through to see the front sight and your target. The peep sight is basically a ring of plastic that holds open a hole in the center of your string. There are two varieties, the kind that sits perpendicular to the string with the string split two, or, three ways around the peep, and the kind that splits the string two ways and has a small rubber tube which is tied to the peep and a cable so that when the bow is drawn the tube is stretched and the peep is perfectly aligned.

I will go over how to situate the peep in the "how to shoot," but you will be best served by having a professional do it for you and having him permanently tie it in.

Along with the two peep varieties they vary in sizes. Peeps with smaller holes are more accurate because you will need to have the back sight 'right on" in order to see through it. There is more variance in how accurate you will be with a bigger peep hole, but a bigger peep hole also lets more light in. More light means you can see through the peep earlier in the morning and later at night. So you want the biggest peep your archery shop has for hunting.

Then you can decide on a peep that uses a rubber tube to always align the peep correctly or one with no tube. Since at every point in this chapter I have recommended fewer parts and/ or fewer moving parts I think you can guess weather or not I like the idea of an additional peep tube.

The next accessory to think about is the "nock." Where the arrow is attached to the string is called the "nocking point." The nocking point will be set on your bow prior to you buying it. The only question is if you want a traditional nock or a "D-loop". The traditional nock is a metal "C" that is clamped to the string and you'll nock your arrow below the metal nock. If you are going to shoot fingers (and be less accurate) you'll want a traditional nock. Almost all new bows today are sold with a length of string tied to the bowstring at the nocking point. With the loop you'll nock your arrow between the two points where the D-loop is tied. The advantage of a D-loop is that you are less likely to twist the bowstring when you attach your release to the back of the loop rather than directly to the string. Two more advantages to d-loops are that the release will wear on the loop not the bow string, and drawing and easing the bow down without firing it can dislodge an arrow with a traditional nock, and that won't happen with a loop.

You will be more accurate with a D-loop. I, however, detest unnecessary additional parts. Every part can go wrong, so the more parts you have the more stuff there is to go wrong.

More stuff = fewer dead deer. More complicated stuff = fewer dead deer. To hell with additional moving and unnecessary stuff.

Next up you need a quiver. A quiver is the thing that attaches your arrows to your bow, and covers up the sharp broadheads. Your choices will include how many arrows your quiver holds (I like more), and what materials the quiver is made out of. Plastic quivers are more prone to make noise when struck by things like branches. Noises alert deer to your presence.

Because I'm giving you novice archers advice, I'm going to tell you to ignore the removal of your quiver. Maybe you can shoot a little better with the quiver removed, but that is one more thing to be concerned about, one more thing to move, one more thing to go wrong...; leave your quiver on your bow all the time, and you'll always know where your next arrow is.

Arrows come in all sorts of varieties and prices. You can buy wood arrows, if you shoot a traditional bow and want to look stylish...or did you want straight arrows? Aluminum arrows have their place, or did, and lots of deer were killed with them, including a few by me. But carbon arrows are lighter and straighter.

For the most part arrow prices increase as the straightness increases. The least expensive arrows are probably fine for shorter distances, and if you're a new archer you may not be able to tell the difference between inexpensive and expensive arrows, for a while anyway.

The feathers, or vanes, on the arrow will number three; two of one color and one of another color. The odd feather, or vane, will stick up or away from the bow when you connect its nock to the string. Feathers were the traditional choice, but the two inch vanes create less drag and are more accurate at longer distances.

The arrows you buy will include a nock, which will be a split piece of plastic at one end of the arrow. You can buy illuminated nocks to replace the standard nocks. The advantage of them is that you might see your arrow's flight a bit better, and a light may help locate an arrow or even a deer if the arrow does not pass through the deer. You'll want green illuminated nocks, not some other color. Remember when I said my green sight pin stays brightest longest? If you get illuminated nocks, get green Nocturnal brand nocks. And make sure that you get the right size for your arrows. Arrows are different sizes and you'll want your nock to fit, because you only pull them out and press them in. Arrow sizes are: S, H, GT, X, etc...

Everybody who I've talked to about lighted nocks has liked them.

Arrows also require an insert. An arrow insert is a metal threaded tube that sticks into the end of the arrow. The insert may stick out to the end or be buried a ways down the end of the arrow. The insert is what you screw your broadheads, and field points into, in order to attach them to the arrow. Inserts will likely come with your arrows.

Your selected arrow may have standard inserts or "Deep Six" inserts. Deep six inserts have finer threads and are advertised as being stronger than the standard inserts. My problem with the deep six inserts is that there are only about three broadheads that

151

you can use with them. I'll recommend standard inserts (which will affect your arrow selection) because you'll be able to find more things that work with them, than you will find parts that are compatible with deep sixes.

Arrows are made at around thirty one inches long and are cut to fit your bow, which, if it's a compound, will be adjusted to fit you. Your arrows will need to be measured, in order to do so, take your bow to where you are going to get your arrows. The arrows will stick out about an inch past the riser (the part of the bow that includes the grip, and to which nearly everything is attached). And then the inserts will be glued, or epoxied into place.

Have a professional measure, cut and glue the inserts in your arrows for you.

You will practice your shooting with a pointy tip screwed into your arrows' inserts. This is known as a field tip. The diameter of them should match your arrow. Any field tip shape will do, but the weight, measured in "grains" is very important.

Arrows, field tips, broadheads, bullets, and gunpowder are measured with a unit of measurement called "grains." The number of grains is the weight of the arrow, or whatever, just like you might be weighed in "pounds" or "kilograms."

First you will select your broadheads, and then you will select your field tips to match the broadheads size.

Broadhead sizes will come in two sizes, for deer hunting: 100 grains in weight, and 125 grains in weight. Lighter broadheads can be shot farther and heavier broadheads deliver more mass to the target. The rough, general rule is to use 125 grain broadheads on "medium" size animals like elk and bears, and 100 grain broadheads on "small" big game animals.

Gene Wensel, in his book "One Man's Whitetail" (which you should read) says that heavier arrows are better for hitting harder.

If you plan to hunt with 100 grain broadheads, then you need to practice with 100 grain field points. And use 125 grain field points with 125 grain broadheads.

There are a huge number of broadheads available. There are way too many styles to cover here, or even to get experience with, but we will cover the broadhead basics.

What you want in a broadhead is: razor sharp blades, which are as wide as possible, sturdy construction, and field point flight ballistics.

Cuts with sharper blades bleed more, and heal more slowly.

The wider your broadhead blades are, the more likely they are to cut a vital organ.

Conical field points have the best possible flight characteristics; anything that is added to them creates drag, which slows arrows, and may cause "planeing," or the curving of the flight path.

Broadheads can be arranged into two categories: fixed and mechanical. Fixed broadheads are two, three, or four bladed razor blades (or similar) that are triangularly shaped and have no moving parts. Mechanical broadheads have two, or three razor blades (or similar) that fold into a cone shape, and open (or deploy) when it hits the target.

The advantages of a fixed blade are that the blades are always ready for contact, no movement is required, and there are fewer parts to break; some are also sharpenable. The advantages for mechanical broadheads are that they are more aerodynamic in flight (read that as "more accurate") and they can be wider than any fixed broadheads on contact.

The ideal fixed-blade broadhead will have: three blades, to prevent planeing, have the widest possible blades, to maximize the odds of hitting vitals, and have a "cut on impact" tip. I shoot 100 grain standard 3 blade Muzzy brand broadheads.

Muzzy brand broadheads have been killing deer for decades. The advantages for the standard three blade Muzzys are the replaceable blades, their history of success, and the fact that the standard 3 blade Muzzy has a 1 3/16" cutting diameter, which is bigger than any fixed blade braodhead but the Ramcat.

Prior to using the 100 grain Muzzys I used broadheads based of the original deer hunting broadhead, "Bear Razorheads." With Bear Razorhead style broadheads, I recovered every buck I ever hit anywhere. The problem with Bear Razorhead style broadheads is that their two main blades act as a sail and they do not fly straight. Long distance shooting is not happening with this style. But my second and third bucks with a bow were hit in the rear hindquarter and both went down inside of fifty yards.

Lots of deer have been killed with the old favorite, and if you plan on hunting with a traditional bow (thanks again for leaving more deer alive for me), then shooting Bear Razorhead style broadheads might not be a bad way to go. Your range with a traditional bow is so short that broadhead planeing will not cause too much damage to your accuracy.

A fixed broadhead is always "open" and ready for cutting. But even three blade fixed broadheads are not as accurate as a broadhead that folds into a cylindrical shape. Really long shooting (longer range than you'll be doing) will almost require shooting with a mechanical broadhead.

The other advantage of mechanical broadheads is the cutting diameter. Two inch wide fixed broadheads are unpractical, and yet common among mechanical broadheads. A bigger cutting diameter gives you more leeway to be off target, and means that you'll be more likely to hit a vital organ.

The disadvantage is that it might not open, or it may open prematurely, or only one side will open and throw your shooting off.

I like the fewest possible moving parts, so I have not shot a mechanical broadhead. As far as I can tell the top brand is: Rage. Rage broadheads have shot lots of deer and are the top known brand in broadheads. They may also be the top brand due to their marketing.

Personally, though, I'm never going to use a mechanical broadhead for deer. If they worked 100% of the time, then maybe; but all mechanical broadheads work some percent of the time less than 100%. That means you will not get some deer because your broadhead fails you.

One more archery item that you'll need is a "release." A release is a hook, or two, with a trigger and a strap which you use to pull and release your bowstring. The traditional method with which to shoot a bow is to have one finger above the arrow, on the string, and two below at the first joint. The problem with shooting "fingers" is that they are not as consistent as they might be. And the trick in shooting a bow well is consistency. Shooting fingers requires those three points of contact on the string. A release has only one point of contact on the string, and that contact will be exactly the same every time.

How a release works will be covered in the next chapter.

The decisions to make on a release are general style preference (Scott or Tru-Ball/ Tru-Fire), belt buckle or Velcro, stick or strap, and one caliper or two.

Scott releases have killed lots of deer and if you like them then that's fine, but they're not for me. Think exceptionally light trigger pull.

That leaves me with Tru-Ball or Tru-Fire releases. Don't get the cheapest one, a bad release once scared me away from all releases for a while, and you don't want that. So expect to spend at least $45 on a release.

The advantage of a Velcro release is its tightness and lack of metal to click on things and make noise. The disadvantage is the noise. The advantage of the buckle is the sturdiness and the quietness, unless you hit the metal buckle against something that makes noise.

I've got a Velcro strap and I put it on and take it off when I'm at my truck, not while up in my tree.

Almost everybody likes the minimal movement that comes from the release being connected to the strap by a stick. Note that some are length adjustable and some are not. I happen to like a strap connecting the release to the wrist strap, because it fits in my hand better, and while I'm hunting my bow is in my left hand and my right hand is wrapped around my release with only my right index finger being needed to move in order to shoot.

Choose a release with two calipers (the hooks that hold the string) not a release with one. A single caliper doesn't release as straight as a two caliper release does.

And one last bow accessory before I forget: buy a bow specific target to shoot at.

The thing with bow accessories is that you are looking for products that always work and do not make noise. Fix or replace things that break. When things go wrong you miss opportunities at deer. And things that make noise are just waiting to scare deer away from you.

33
Shooting a Bow

Before we get to shooting a bow, let me point out that shooting a bow without an arrow in it is known as a "dry-fire." With a dry-fire the energy used in pulling the bow pack is not transferred to the arrow and instead vibrates the bow all around. Dry-firing can destroy bows, so don't pull a bow back without an arrow in it.

I am going to go over how to shoot a compound bow. Traditional bows are cool, and shoot differently, but they are less effective than compound bows.

We used to shoot bows by pulling the string back with our fingers. Shooting fingers will mean first putting the arrow's nock as far onto the string as it goes, and just below the metal nock. Then you'll put one finger above and two below the arrow and metal nock. (Some do this upside down.) The string will sit in the first joint of your fingers.

However, shooting a bow without a mechanical release will greatly reduce your accuracy. What a release does is provides a consistent single point of contact with the sting. Multiple points on the string, like when we shoot fingers, makes it too easy to move the string side to side, and we are less likely to release the bow cleanly.

With a release and no D-loop, the arrangement will be (from top to bottom) metal nock, then arrow nock, then release. With a release and a D-loop, the arrangement will be: the arrow nock between the two knots of the D-loop and the release hooked to the back of the D-loop. In either case the release's trigger should be pointed away from your face.

Your feet should be shoulder with apart and evenly balanced. You want to stand perpendicular to the target, with you left side (if you're right handed) facing the target.

You should be standing straight up comfortably. Anything that is not smooth and comfortable will though your shooting off.

When your feet are in position and you're standing straight, you'll want to turn your head towards the target.

Then your left hand will hold the bow grip just strongly enough to not drop the bow. A tight grip will throw off your shooting. When your bow is drawn back you do not actually need to hold the bow, you can merely be pushing it away from you. Many guys think this, but then hold the bow with an open hand and then grab it as they shoot so they don't drop it. This is another good way to screw up your shooting.

The open hand technique can be done well, but it almost never is.

With many drop-away arrow rests you'll want your index finger to stick out over the arrow, and just touch it. Arrows can hop off their rests and keeping your finger just lightly touching the arrow will keep it in place.

I will point out again, though, that this is one more thing that you need to do, and therefore one more thing to go wrong. Use a whisker biscuit arrow rest for hunting to minimize problems.

Your left arm should be almost, but not quite, straight out. If your string hits your left arm, you are holding the bow incorrectly.

While you hunt, your arm getting stung on your shot is no big deal, because it will only hurt after the only shot you'll likely get anyway.

You'll want to draw your bow, by pulling the string with your right hand and pushing away with your left. Ideally, the arrow's knock will be in the corner of your mouth when the bow is fully drawn. Some guys like their nose tip to be touching the string so that they draw their string to the same place every time.

And the big trick in shooting a bow well is doing everything the same way every time.

When your bow is drawn back you want to feel your hand against your face. You want to feel the same bones in your face with the same parts of your hand the same way every time.

Where you hold your right hand on your face is called your "anchor point". It needs to be the exact same place every time in order to shoot well. Many first time archers, particularly girls, do not hold their right hand tight to their face; but you need to in order to shoot well.

A compound bow has its draw length adjusted to fit your arm length. When you buy your bow the bow shop will set adjust your bow to your draw length for you.

Adult compound bows will usually have a ten pound adjustment you can make in it draw weight, generally 50-60lbs or 60-70ibs. A bow will shoot best near the top of its draw weight range, but if you cannot pull the bow back comfortably then you may not be able to pull it back when you need to. It will be harder to pull back when its cold out.

Pull as much weight as you can with ease.

One advantage of a compound bow is its "let-off." A bow's let-off occurs because a compound bow has cams and not two wheels on the end of the limbs. When you pull the bow "over the hump" you actually only be holding something like 20 or 25% of your bow's peak draw weight. This is useful when you pull the bow back and then need to hold it for a bit while you wait for the deer to reposition itself.

Feet square, shoulder width apart, weight evenly balanced on both feet, perpendicular to the target, bow held loosely, and drawn back to the corner of your mouth, feel your face with your hand the same way every time.

You'll want to be looking through your peep sight. Your bow shop should set it to the correct height for you.

Some guys like to point out that they like a round front sight guard so that the round peep hole to lines up with the round front sight guard. I never bother with that, but if it helps , it helps.

You want to look through the peep, but you don't want to look at the peep, just know that its there. You should be able to notice a gray blur when you look through it.

If you have multiple pins on your bow sight the top sight will be the close one. My top pin is set to targets twenty yards away. Most bow shots happen around sixteen yards away so many guys set their first pin for sixteen yards. And any additional sight pins will set at ten yard increments longer than your first pin.

The advantage of your first pin being on at sixteen yards is that your top pin is set for most shots that you'll take. The advantage of your first pin being on at twenty yards is that your bottom pin will be better positioned for further shots.

With a compound bow you will want to squeeze the trigger not jerk it. Squeeze like a rifle, not jerk like a shotgun.

As you shoot your bow you'll want to practice with the goal of having every arrow touch each other once it hits the target. Aim the same place, and hit the same place. If your bow was set up well, then you'll only need to adjust your front sight in order to get the arrows to hit right where you are aiming.

You'll sight your top pin in at fifteen or twenty yards and then the rest should fall into place at ten yard increments. Shoot several arrows before moving your sight. If you aim at the same place and one arrow goes right and one goes left, then your bow isn't well set up, or you're a bad shot. If you shoot arrows and they all go left, then move the sight left. If your arrows all go high, then move your sight up. And so on.

34

Hunting Accessories

Besides clothing, a weapon, and a tree stand, there are a few other hunting accessories that you'll want to have with you.

A knife is an essential piece of deer hunting equipment.

Knives are needed for field dressing, skinning, removing meat, cutting open the packaging for other equipment, etc.

There are many uses for knives and essentially infinite knife options. Lots of knives are cool and interesting. You can always make up an excuse to get another knife. I always keep one in my car as an emergency tool. I also carry a small spare in my camouflage pants. A pocketknife was always carried by our grandfathers and you might be surprised at how often a pocket knife is useful when you carry one around. I also keep a knife in my bow case, because I can.

What sort of knife should you get for deer hunting?

My uncle, who is more knowledgeable on the subject than I am, doesn't care what knife he uses so long as it is sharp.

Knives made out of poor metal will not hold a sharp edge for long and are more dangerous than knives made out of quality metals.

I'm afraid that I don't know which knives are made out of quality metals and which ones are not. I do know that if you get a knife made by a brand like: Buck, Gerber, Kershaw, or SOG then you will likely have a quality knife, even if you paid little for it.

Your deer hunting knife should have a blade around 3-4" long. A shorter blade will mean that you will be required to do more work in any cutting job. Smaller blades will also be more likely to break than bigger ones.

You don't want a blade that is too much bigger than 3-4" because one job your hunting knife will do is to field dress a deer. Field dressing requires having the whole knife inside of the chest of the deer. A really big knife will be too big to be maneuverable.

The height of the blade and the shape of the blade make certain jobs easier or harder. To fillet fish you want a long thin blade, and to field dress deer I quite like the thick and tall blade on my knife. I don't know much more than that about blade shapes. I say: knives are cool and cheap, buy a bunch and try them all to find the one that you like best.

There is really only one decision that you need to make: fixed or folding.

A folding Buck model 110 is the standard deer hunting knife and it has been used for decades. I used one for about ten years. Folding knives are good because they can be folded into a small item without an exposed blade and without need of a sheath. A folding knife can be slipped into any pocket and you should get one, at least, as your backup.

Any time I hear from, or read, a knife expert they point to the ease of carry you get with a folding knife, but they invariably prefer fixed blades. A fixed blade knife is sturdier and stronger than any folding knife can be. The first time I field dressed a deer with a fixed blade knife I was very much impressed with how much easier it was to work with. The big disadvantage of a fixed blade knife is that it requires a sheath; without one you are carrying an exposed blade. If you get a fixed blade knife, then there is no point in getting anything other than one with a full tang. The tang of a knife is the part of the metal of which some is the blade, and the tang is located inside, or between the handle. There are a variety of tang types, but a full tang will be stronger and sturdier than any other style. Recognize a knife with a full tang by noticing that the piece of metal, of which part is the blade, extends to the butt of the knife and the handle is two pieces of another material attached to either side of the metal.

So what you want for your hunting knife is a quality knife, with a 3-4″ blade, and preferably a fixed blade model. You should also have a spare, at least in your car, because knives do break and they can get dirty when you need a clean one. I recommend getting a fixed blade knife for your main use and a folder to keep as a spare.

Expect to spend $20-200 on a hunting knife.

The standard Buck Model 110 Folding Hunter costs $47 and is always a good choice.

I am currently using a Rough Rider Wood Hunter. Its very cheap at $20, but I have zero complaints after using it on around six deer so far. I quite like it.

Possibly, you could survive with only the equipment found in their specific chapters and a knife, but there are other things that can be useful.

A length of rope is useful for tying deer to the top of your car, pulling your weapon up to your treestand after you, and some people like to drag deer out of the woods by pulling them with a rope. A ¼ to 3/8 inch diameter rope can be used for the above tasks. If you are going to use a rope to pull your weapon up your tree after you then it will need to be at least as long as your height up the tree, plus a few extra feet.

Thicker ropes tangle less. You may also want to use a lighter to singe the ends to keep it from unraveling if you cut it.

Some hunters like to keep one rope with them and carry it to each tree. Other hunters, who hunt multiple fixed position stands, may keep a rope tied to each stand to pull weapons up. Don't use a brightly colored rope if you are going to leave one always up at each stand. And don't leave that scent collecting rope hanging at deer nose level. I prefer to have one rope and keep it with me, because I always have it, and because its one less human thing to leave around the deer.

Flashlights are useful for going to, or from treestands, in the dark. Take two if getting lost might become a serious problem. The flashlights with LED s give better light for blood trailing deer, they are much better than standard flashlights.

Your cell phone, if it works in the woods, can be used to call for help, etc. Don't use it to take pictures of deer or text people, or leave the ringer on. All of those things will make it easier for the deer to detect you and should therefore be avoided.

I'm not going to go beyond flashlights and your cell phone for safety precautions. Take care to be safe while out in the woods, and you may be well served to learn about surviving in the wilderness because anything can happen. Wilderness survival is beyond the scope of this book. Take special care if there is any chance that you could get lost or unable to leave the woods.

Reflective flagging tape, or some other reflective item, can help you to make your way to a stand in the dark.

Deer calls, scents and decoys can be used to bring deer in closer to you. These things can help, if you know how to use them, but I don't recommend getting any of these things until you have some experience hunting and know what to expect everywhere else. These attractants are not magic, or shortcuts, they will not even bring a buck to your tree from a very long ways away. What you'll hope for with these items is that a deer will come a few yards closer than it would have without these items being used. If you hunt where there are deer, then sooner or later one will walk by you.

If you are here and deer are there, then your best bet is to move there, your next best bet is to make here more like there, and your final option is to use scents and calls to bring the deer closer.

Once you have the rest of the ideas in this book figured out, then you may want to add these attractants to slightly improve your hunting experience. They can help fine tune your hunting, but you are not likely to see vast improvements because of them. Some hunters may argue with this idea, but to that I say that first you should figure the basics (this book) and then move on to advanced hunting skills (beyond this book's scope) after you have the basics figured out.

One exception to my recommendation for not bothering with scents is to use scent killing sprays, or soaps, or shampoos, or laundry detergents. All of these hunting specific scent killers reduce the amount that you smell. People smell quite a bit to a deer and its possible that even your shampoo might be enough to alert a deer to your presence. Find the scent killing items in your sporting goods store and use them as directed.

Trail cameras have their own chapter and I'll repeat here that you, a beginning hunter should skip them unless you have money to burn and are prepared to follow the same stealthy procedures in visiting the cameras as you do while hunting.

Food plot equipment also has its own chapter, and I'll say here that you can skip that stuff until you have a plan for improving your hunting property.

Gutting gloves are very helpful when field dressing deer. Some hunters may look down on you for wearing gloves for filed dressing, but wearing them means that you won't need to wash your hands or arms as soon as you are done. What you'll look for, in a sporting goods store are packages that contain orange gloves that go past your elbow and latex gloves to go tightly over the loose orange gloves.

Removing the end of the large intestine from within the pelvis can be made easier with a tool of some kind. You may get a plastic tool called a "butt out" to pull the tube out, or you might get a small saw of some sort to split a small bone in the pelvis. You might skip getting this tool to see what you need after you've field dressed your first deer, and then buy something once you know what to expect.

A meat saw can be useful in butchering deer and removing antlers. Many people prefer the taste of meat from deer butchered with only knives because the saws add bone grit to the meat, but saws can be useful too.

Considering how many headless road killed deer I've seen, I suspect that many road killed bucks lose their antlers to guys that carry meat saws around with them. This is illegal in many places. Check your local laws.

A soft measuring tape, usually used for making clothes, or a length of string and a ruler, or yardstick, are all the tools you'll need to score your deer antlers.

A length of twine or thick string may also be useful for tying your deer tag to your dead deer, or for other purposes. I always have about a foot of twine with me for whatever purpose comes along.

35

Where to Spend and Where to Save

There are a lot of hunting things you may buy in order to help you hunt deer. Where should you save money? Where should you spend?

Spend money on land. Having a good hunting property can make every aspect of deer hunting better. Spend what you can on acquiring good land. This may be buying a property, leasing a property, or asking a land owner for permission to hunt.

You should do what it takes in order to be safe while hunting. It may cost a bit but you shouldn't be cheap with safety harnesses or replacing tree stand straps.

Sights are important. Think of it this way: every dollar extra you spend on scopes or bow sights may add a minute to the shooting light at the beginning and end of each day. And the big bucks usually move right at dawn and dusk when all the shooting light you can get is helpful.

Your bullets and arrows are what kill the deer. Don't be cheap when you buy your ammunition and arrows. These projectiles are expected to travel very fast through the air and hit a specific target. Any irregularity among them can cause them to go off course, and hitting a deer is hard enough as it is.

For archery releases or release aids are important, throw away rusty releases. My first experience with a release was with a cheap release that would open if you shook it. This scared me away from all releases for quite a few years. My current release from Tru Ball costs about seventy dollars.

Whisker Biscuit arrow rests are the way to go, even though they don't cost much. Spend on one of my two favorite pieces of hunting equipment. They are not particularly expensive but do not get a cheaper arrow rest for hunting. The least expensive Whisker Biscuit ($40) is fine.

Comfort is important. For example: my feet get cold easily so I cannot get cheap boots and expect to stay out in the cold. Example two: a cheap treestand may be small which will result in your discomfort and becoming anxious to end your hunts early. Or a cheap stand may be way too heavy and cause pain when setting it up. Don't try to save money on treeestands; get the best that you can afford.

You can save some money on guns. A gun needs to put the bullet, or slug, where you want it every time. But they do not need to be really expensive. You could spend $400 to $3000 on a new rifle, but your father's old one probably works fine. You may even buy a quality used one for a couple hundred dollars. It just needs to hit where you aim and rifles are really very simple. Buy an inexpensive bolt action rifle in .270 Win, .30-06, or .308 Win and you should be set for nearly any whitetail deer hunting situation. Do not try to save money on a rifle scope. Buy the best that you can afford. You will not regret buying a Swarovski, or Schmidt & Bender rifle scope. They are worth every penny.

You could spend a couple hundred dollars on expensive name brand camouflage, but if you're looking to save money, then buy whatever inexpensive camoflage that breaks up your outline, and spray it with a UV killer and a scent killer. Once you've used UV killer on your camouflage almost anything that is dark in color and has a varied color scheme should work fine.

The purpose of camouflage is to break up your outline and possibly reduce your smell.

Ideally, perhaps, you'll have a light suit of camoflage, a medium suit of camoflage, and a heavy suit of camoflage, and an orange suit of camoflage for when the temperatures, and seasons, change. Instead, you can save money buy buying one light to medium camoflage suit that is several sizes too big and adding and removing layers underneath. Get it in the standard green /brown colors and merely add a cheap orange vest and an orange hat over the top when the season's laws change.

Having an ATV can be great and add a lot to your hunting, but they are unnecessary and expensive. There are ways to work around having one, like hiring someone to plant your food plots for you.

Trail cameras can be great to have, but I don't like them. The cheapest one you'd want to buy costs around $150. And that's for something where you'll need quite a few of them, and they'll be obsolete in a few years. Many hunters who are serious about scent control while hunting think nothing of checking cameras while wearing street clothes and smeely tennis shoes. The reason that I don't like trail cameras is because I don't think you should be walking around on your hunting property any more than you have to. Once you know you have bucks and an idea for where they live on your property, forget the trail cameras. If you are going to use trail cameras put them 8 – 10 feet up so they aren't right in the deers line of sight and smell.

Cabins and sheds are great, but if you already have a garage and want to save money stick your stuff in the garage. But be careful to keep your hunting stuff away from any stuff that smells like gas. Don't in any case, build your cabin or shed in the middle of your property. Put one in a corner of your property.

Some people swear by having binoculars. If you hunt out west at long ranges, a pair will be necessary. Swarovskis are the best, Zeiss, Leupold, and Vortex make good stuff too. You want the Swarovskis because they will allow you to see for many more minutes in the dawn and dusk when lesser stuff will not have the light necessary to work. Because deer move the most at dawn and dusk, every extra minute that you get will help a lot. If you are just getting started, or just need a pair of binoculars, then spend around $220 on a pair of Vortex Diamondback 8x42. While writing this book I worked part-time selling bows and binoculars in a sporting goods store, and I have never heard anything bad about Vortex or any of its stuff. And 8x42 is the size you want for whitetail deer hunting, no matter what kind of binoculars you want while hunting.

Rangefinders can be great; you are made of money aren't you? Practice shooting at different ranges and estimate the distances. Although if you are going to hunt out west and plan on taking very long shots you'll want a rangefinder. You could spend as much as you want on a rangefinder, but if I were going to get one I'd buy the Vortex Ranger 1000 ($380) because it will do all that needs doing and it has a lifetime warranty. Spending less and needing to replace your electronic device (which are not known for reliability) every few years will end up costing a lot more in the long run than buying a good one with a lifetime warranty once.

Calls, attracting scents, and decoys can be the difference between shooting a buck and not shooting a buck. Many bucks have been shot with the aid of these products, but how many opportunities have been lost because a buck noticed their setup, or their operation was not ideal? For the most part, a scent, call, or decoy will, maybe, bring a buck that is a hundred yards away, a bit closer to you. But don't overdo it. If you call too much, he'll see that although you're making the right sound, you're not a deer. Anyway this book is for fundamentals. All of these things are beyond fundamentals.

A 10 foot Hooeyman tree saw ($90) is a great too to have and I use one every time I hang a stand up.

A particularly useful point of information for those of you new to hunting equipment is to notice which products include the names of TV shows on them, or even use the TV show name for the product name. A hunting product prominently noting a TV show as the product's name is almost certainly...junk.

The product may be mediocre if you are lucky, but I'd skip anything with a TV show name on it. A company that uses TV show names to name its products needs to pay that show, which is fine, but that means the money going into that show is not money that is going into, say, better materials.

I'd even skip whole brands that use this marketing technique. You'll never see a Swarovski The TV Show X riflescope or the Lone Wolf TV Show Y climbing treestand. These companies spend more money on creating good products rather than just marketing them.

On a similar note, things that don't need to be camouflage, like binoculars, can sometimes come with a camoflage option for a few dollars more. This is not as bad as the TV show name products, but is unnecessary. If you buy the camo option rather than standard black, or whatever, I will laugh at you for wasting money.

If a product is not mentioned in this book, you almost certainly don't need it, with exceptions for your specific injuries, health or comfort. If its not mentioned, then I don't have it, and get along fine without it.

And to conclude this chapter, my last point will be to point out that the worst piece of equipment that you can buy is one of those racks thats sticks out the back of your truck's reciver. Way too many times I've seen people hauling deer on those racks only to see the horns or legs being worn off by bieng dragged along the road. Never buy one of those racks.

36

Stealth

If a deer knows that you're out in the woods, then it's going to avoid you.

Like people, deer have five senses. A deer isn't likely to touch or taste you so we won't concern ourselves with that. This leaves us with sight, scent, and sound.

The best way for a deer to detect you with its eyes is for you to move. Since you'll be hunting from a stand usually, you want to be comfortable to prevent your fidgeting and movement. An uncomfortable seat is unacceptable. In one of the tree stand chapters I pointed out that stands that require their foam seat cushions are unacceptable because you will be uncomfortable when you don't use that stupid cushion.

When you are hunting you'll be sitting mostly still while waiting for signs of deer. You obviously do not want to move too much, or too quickly. All of your movements should be slow and controlled. You can limit your movement by paying attention to where your treestands are facing. As I said in a previous chapter, ideally your left side will face the target, but your front should be where most of the action occurs, so you see them before they see you.

Another thing to keep in mind is that once a deer is looking your way you don't want to move. There will be times when you want to be twisted around to see behind you . Many times you'll be twisted into an uncomfortable position when you need to freeze. There's not much you can do about that, but you should be conscious of when you are in positions you cannot freeze in.

In order to avoid being seen by deer you should wear camouflage clothes that are not washed in normal detergent, and sprayed with UV killer on occasion, or washed in UV killing detergent.

Do also keep in mind that you do not want to be silhouetted against the sky when you are up in your tree. Trees that are full of leaves when you put your stand up may not give you cover when the leaves fall down.

Finally, for sight, avoid wearing or using things that are shiny. Paint your treestand chains black, don't use your phone when it's dark, and so on.

Next we want to avoid being smelled by the deer.

I've never paid as much attention to smells as I should. But I am careful to do things like taking showers, wearing clean clothes, and washing my hands just before hunting. Deer can't smell you if you are down wind.

If you leave something that got you smelly, obviously you need to de-stink. For the most part not smelling mostly means not doing things that contribute to your smells. Don't wear cologne, don't use smelly shampoo, don't pump gas the day you hunt, don't eat food that makes your breath smell, and so on.

One place many hunters do very badly on their scent control is to wear their hunting clothing outside of the woods. Wearing your hunting boots across a gas station parking lot can do nothing but compile people related smells. Wearing your camouflage coat to the store can do nothing but accumulate people smells. It amazes me how many camouflage coats with back tags I see in bars. You will not see good deer hunters wearing their hunting clothing outside of the woods.

Scent killing sprays can help, but mostly you want to be living minimally scented during the hunting season. Many guys even become vegetarians during the hunting season because vegetarians smell differently than carnivores do.

One last place many hunters fail on their scent killing is sweating on their way into their stands. Wearing heavy hunting clothes is hot when you walk in to your tree. Walk slowly, and wait to put your coat on until you get to your tree.

The minimum you need to do is limit your accumulation of smells before you hunt. Keeping your hunting clothes in scent proof bags is also a good idea. Minimize your smells.

Deer trust their noses more than anything, but nothing gets a deer's attention like making noise. To avoid making noise you should clear the trails into your stands, walk in and out slowly, and don't talk loud, or slam car doors. Turning your phone off is something you'll forget to do on occasion. (I miss quite a few calls during the fall because my phone is on silent, not vibrate, but silent.)

Your hunting accessories shouldn't make any noise. Stands that creak are making metallic noises unusual in nature. And things like metal zippers, and buckles on your bow release can click when hit together.

One more point before I conclude this chapter. Going to your stand late, leaving early, and not being quiet after your hunt are all fine ways to let the deer know where you are. If you are going into your stand late, you might seriously consider not going in at all.

Move slowly, don't accumulate smells before you hunt, and fix anything that has the potential to make noise and you'll be set to go undetected from the deer.

37

The Deer's Seasons

Ideally, you'll hunt as much as possible. The more you hunt the more deer you see. The more deer you see the more bucks you see. The more bucks you see the more you get a shot at. The more bucks you get a shot at the more big bucks you get a shot at.

But we can't spend all our time hunting deer. Work and other considerations take away from hunting time. (Or so I've heard.)

A deer's seasons are different from ours. Theirs seem to be based around the winter. During the winter food is hard to come by and weak deer die. And so does give birth to fawns early in the spring so that its not too cold out for the young fawns and so they have a full summer and fall to prepare for their first winter.

I going to say that there are five deer hunting seasons. In Wisconsin there are several seasons (early archery, firearm, muzzleloader, youth-hunt, etc.), but I mean seasons as the deer see it.

The main thing to understand about deer hunting seasons is the rut. The rut is when the does are in heat (ready to mate). They are only in heat for a few days. This is so the fawns are born in the spring and then have all spring, summer, and fall to grow big before the next winter.

So you may read in books and magazines about: the pre-rut, the rut, and the post-rut. Here in Wisconsin the early archery and youth hunt occur before the pre-rut really begins. During this time you will likely see only does and small bucks. They will be traveling between their bedding areas and their feeding areas. If your goal is big bucks, then you will be hunting this "pre-pre-rut" with only a hope of getting lucky. During this time you will hunt more for the enjoyment of being out rather than actually expecting to shoot a big buck. But big bucks are shot very early, and I shot my first buck with a bow, a 125" – 9point, on the first day of the early archery season. I shot my last buck with a bow on October 5th. Bucks can be shot before and after the rut.

During the pre-rut you will begin to see more deer activity. The bucks will be on the lookout for hot does. They will be rubbing trees with their antlers, making scrapes, and fighting each other.

A "rub" will be a smaller tree that has about a foot's (1') worth of its bark removed from one side. You may often see a worn smooth part on a buck's antlers between the pedicle and first point. A line of rubs can show you when the buck passed through the area, because a deer will not be turning a round to rub. If you stand with your back to the bedding areas (thickest, most impenetrable stuff) and you see the rubs in front of you leading towards a big area of food, then the buck(s) that made the rubs were wandering from their bedding and towards the food. We know that deer are bedded during the day and head out to eat at dusk, therefore rubs in this way are showing us that the buck(s) passed by in the evening. And the rubs will be seen heading towards the bedding areas for bucks making them in the morning going from the food to the cover.

The purpose of a rub is to work out aggression for the bucks. Rubs often show up in lines (multiple rubs on a line of trees). These are not as hunt-able as scrapes, but they do show that there are bucks around and they are moving around, looking for does.

Scrapes are patches of ground that have all grass and leaves "scraped" away by a deer's front hooves. Scrapes will be located under thin branches that are about your chest, or head, height. The bucks break a small branch over the scrape and rub the broken branch with their heads and leave their scent. The plan is that there will be a bunch of scrapes made on, or near, trails and when a doe is in heat she will urinate in the scrape. Then the bucks will walk over the scrape occasionally and smell for the hot doe.

Gene Wensel, in his book "One Man's Whitetail" (which you should read), says that the first rubs and scrapes of the season are made by the biggest bucks in the area.

During this pre-rut the bucks will be looking for hot does. You will begin to see the bigger bucks because they spend more time looking for does and less time hiding or as nocturnal animals. The bucks will chase the does but the does will always run away.

This is when scents and calls will be most effective. The bucks will be looking, listening, and smelling for any kind of sign that there is a hot doe around. You may also see bucks fighting during the pre-rut.

During the few days of the rut the biggest bucks will be out and about and the bucks and does will be moving around much more. During the peak of the rut the bucks and does will be running around very early. They will be running literally at full speed, much of the time. Often you will see multiple bucks chasing one hot doe. The peak night is often the most exciting time to be out.

If you are only able to hunt for a few days of the year then you want to hit the peak of the rut, several days before, and a few days after. Take your vacation days from the pre-rut through the

177

rut. Figure out when they happen, and each geographic location will have its rut at a different time. The rut occurs in the first week of November in central Wisconsin, and, I think, in December in Texas. The timing depends on the timing for the following winter when the fawns should be six months old, or older.

After the rut comes the post-rut. The post-rut is similar to the pre-rut. During both times the bucks will be looking for any sign of a hot doe that they can find. While the rut is happening calls and scents will not compare to the actual does, but before and after the rut calls and scents can help get a buck's attention.

During the "post-post-rut" you will once again just be hoping to get lucky. Once all of the does are out of heat for the season, a deer's priority will be to eat a lot before the coming winter. This is the time when baiting is most effective, especially if where you hunt has snowy winters and food is hard to find.

I don't hunt much past the post-rut. By that time I will have hunted a lot for the year already, the big bucks will not be seen much, and in Wisconsin, it gets cold in December.

38

The Entrance

Entering your stand is very important. Making lots of noise sweating, flashing lights all over walking through bedding areas, etc will all prevent you from shooting deer.

The first thing to consider when you are going to be hunting; the options are: the morning, the evening, both, or all day. (Note that your local laws may determine when you are allowed to hunt. You may get to your tree early, but perhaps you are required to have your weapon cased until the "appropriate" time.)

A morning hunt should have you in your stand about an hour before sunrise, but earlier is better. That means you should know how long it takes to get to your stand and start walking towards it that much early.

Earlier is better, but in the other hand, being up your tree too early will tire you which will cause you to fidget more and your scent will have more time to encompass your area.

Being up in your tree a hour before sunrise gives time for the woods to settle down after your entrance and before the deer arrive. Arriving too late can have you still walking in when the deer come through. Even if you are a few minutes ahead of the deer you'll be moving and making noise as soon as you are up your tree; adjusting the gun or bow, and putting a face mask on, etc. After an hour the squirrels and birds should resume their activities near you too.

An hour before sunrise is a good time to be up your tree, but if you know your neighbor's schedule then you may want to change your entrance time to be ahead of him.

When you enter the woods you'll be moving and making noise. When you do that the deer will notice you and move out of your way. So if your neighbor starts hunting at six you'll want to be settled in your stand at five. That way the deer will move away from your late neighbor and towards the quiet area that you are in.

Being the quiet area of the woods can be a huge advantage if your neighbors unintentionally move the deer towards you.

An evening hunt should have you settled in your tree at least two and a half hours before sunset; earlier is better.

And an all-day hunt will combine the two.

Some of you will need to park along public roads in order to get to your hunt. If you need to do this then I suggest not having camoflage details or hunting related stickers on your truck. If your truck look like it belongs to a hunter and its always parked in the same spot, then other guys driving by may decide that they know where a good place to hunt is too.

Being quiet when hunting starts by not slamming car doors and not talking loudly when you arrive. You don't need to announce to the deer that you have arrived.

Now would be a good time to make sure that your phone is off.

Another thing I do is to turn off all of the interior lights in my truck. Lighting up the area around your truck every time you enter and leave it cannot be good.

The path to your stand is best cleared of brush and dead leaves before you hunt. You'll want to be as silent as possible when entering the woods, and nothing makes noise like walking on dead leaves.

The best way to arrange your clothing upon entrance is to carry it to your tree, so that you don't sweat in it, and then put it on at the base of your tree. Don't make the mistake of leaving a warm article of clothing on the ground after a warm walk in. You may want that coat when it gets colder later in the evening and clothing left on the ground is something that the deer will notice and become more wary of its surroundings.

My entrance is conducted as follows: 1) arrive in car 2) remove camouflage clothing from car 3) put camouflage pants and boots on 4) put Velcro arrow release on wrist (during archery season) 5) retrieve weapon from car 6) walk to my stand 7) put on coat 8) climb tree

I have pointed out that the trick in being successful is hunting a lot, but that does not mean hunting one stand every day. If you are at one place often enough the deer will eventually leave the area where you always are.

Take special care when entering the woods. Spooking deer before you get there just wastes the day's hunt and alerts deer to where you like to be.

Bushnell Ⓜ Camera Name 29.12Inʃ 60°F ●   11-21-2012 15.21:24

39

The Hunt

The hunt is boring.

On opening day of the 2001 Wisconsin archery season I thought about how boring it is to sit in one place and not move for hours. To have one view and not move is dull. And a half hour later I shot a buck with my bow and reconsidered the boredom.

Then there are the annoyances, such as mosquitoes, and the fact that a squirrel hopping sounds a lot like a deer taking one step. You'll turn to look and see a squirrel, and look again and again only to see another stupid squirrel. But you can't stop looking or that one time you don't look a buck will evade your detection.

You can stave off some boredom by reading a book. The additional movement, distraction from your task, and white pages are all liable to prevent you from shooting a deer. But if you need something to hold your attention while in your stand, then I'll recommend a Kindle from amazon.com. A kindle is not bright white, you can turn pages with less movement, slip it into your pocket more easily, and you can get a lot of classic books for free.

Keeping your phone on you is good as a safety measure, but it is a tempting distraction. Texting and picture taking can be amusing but it adds movement and noise, two things you don't want while trying to be stealthy.

Be sure to at least turn your ringer off.

I don't recommend reading, texting, or picture taking while hunting which leaves you with few options for entertainment.

Spend the time thinking. Not seeing deer is boring, but I look forward to spending several hours with only the option to think.

You can think about whatever you like, but if shooting a buck is your goal, then thinking about where the deer are coming and going to and from, and thinking about which nearby trees would make better stands is the optimum use of your brain's time.

If you see a lot of deer moving eighty yards to your left, then you can look for a tree sixty or a hundred yards away.

Moving stand locations is what I prefer to think about while up in a tree, but my dad prefers to plan all the food plot and other property improvements for the next season when he's hunting.

If nothing else you can watch the leaves fall from the trees, I always enjoy doing so.

So, you're in your stand and thinking about stuff. Its time for an important question: sit or stand; which is best?

The benefit of sitting is that you will be more comfortable and sit more still. Not moving will mean that you will spook fewer deer. So by sitting you can stay comfortable longer and spook fewer deer.

The bad part of sitting in a tree stand is that you cannot shoot behind you or to your right (if you are right handed).

The benefit of standing is that you can very easily move to shoot in any direction around the tree, except for straight behind you.

And the downside is that by standing for several hours you will get uncomfortable and fidget more than you would were you sitting. The fidgeting will be noticeable by deer and fewer of them will come close to you.

Which is best?

Both have a good point and a bad point. I don't know which is best, but I do know what is worst. If you sit for a while, then stand, then sit, etc., then sooner or later, a deer will catch you halfway between sitting and standing and you will need to freeze to avoid spooking the deer.

Pick one: sit or stand, and stick with it.

While standing, or sitting, in your stand, you'll need to have your equipment prepared, and being watching for the deer.

Even if you don't think that you are moving much, any movement can alert a deer to your presence. Scratching your head may be all the movement it takes for a deer to see you. And while a doe will let everyone know when she sees something she doesn't

183

like a big buck will just disappear. I'm sure that there have been many times I have moved just enough for a buck to see me and silently disappear, but I'll never know when that occurs. So keep your movement to a minimum, particularly if there is no breeze and nothing is moving at all.

The correct time to not be moving is whenever you can, and as often as you can. Things like planning around the weather or (heaven forbid) moon phases means that you'll just think yourself out of hunting on some days. Missing days is a good way to not shoot any deer.

Light rains, light winds, and any amount of snow fall should not prevent you from hunting. The first light snow of the year is often an excellent time for deer activity.

Heavy winds and torrential rainfall will make sitting uncomfortable and likely prevent the deer from moving, but even then, you should still hunt if it is during the pre-rut, rut, or post-rut.

The only times to miss days in the woods is when the weather seriously threatens your safety.

There is a big exception to the rule of hunting all the time, always. If you hunt one spot too much the deer will know that there is often a hunter there and they'll avoid that spot. I'm constantly amazed with how many people who hunt but have exactly one tree. Even if you move only fifty yards away, and hunt two spots you should have significantly better hunting when the deer don't know exactly where you'll be. In a perfect world, you'd hunt all day every day in the fall and never hunt the same place twice. That isn't really possible or practical, but you should understand that moving to different spots will give you a better chance to avoid the deer's detection.

If you only have one place to hunt on your private land, then you should re-read my chapter on public land in order to find an additional place to hunt.

It has happened way too often to be a coincidence that the first time that I sat in a tree was the time that I shot a buck from it. My first buck with a bow was shot on the opening day of the archery season from a climbing treestand and a tree I'd never sat in before. The first buck shot from the property that I currently hunt was shot from a stand that my uncle had possibly hunted once before, and it was the first time I'd ever sat there. The first buck I shot from over a food plot was shot the very first time that I sat there. My thirteen pointer was shot the first time I had sat in a stand over that area. The buck I shot, and had previously let go elsewhere, which was the one sided four pointer with the left antler pointing down rather than up was the first time I had hunted within 200 yards of that area. The buck I shot while writing this book was shot about 75 yards to the east of any stand I had hunted on any day before. That stand 75 yards to the east was first hunted by me on January 1st of 2010 and I had six bucks walk single file and the spooked when my new coat sounded like Velcro when I leaned away from the tree. It was possibly the first time hunting from the tree 75 yards behind My Favorite Tree when I missed my first buck with a recurve bow. The first time that I ever shot at, and missed, a buck with a bow might have been my first time sitting in My Favorite Tree. I saw five bucks that night, two were two far away and I missed or otherwise flubbed the other three. I missed a 140+ B&C buck the first time that I sat in the big tower my dad and I built.

So of the 25 bucks that I have shot, as of this writing, 6 were shot from a tree on the first time that I hunted there. That's not a coincidence. Sitting in a good spot, even repeatedly, is always a good idea, but there is something to be said for sitting in new places.

An interesting idea may be to have a property, and hunt only one quarter of it each year, and move that quarter with each year. Most deer won't get to be 3 ½ years old so if your rotate through your property every four years, then most deer will never live old enough to ever know that the place where they live is ever hunted. I said in an earlier chapter that you should pick your thickest cover and never enter there, because then the deer will always have a place to feel safe on your property. If you only hunt a rotating quarter of your property every four years the deer may well feel safe throughout your property.

If you have only one spot, then find another, and always keep trying new places. I've done quite well trying new spots.

Before I end this chapter, I want to tell you that you need to keep your eyes moving. Even if you see a deer walk behind a tree it won't always pop out on the other side, it might reappear fifty yards from where you last saw it. I don't know how, but a three foot long deer can disappear behind a six inch tree.

Always keep your eyes moving.

40

The Exit

Sometimes hunting is boring. Not seeing any deer can be boring. Spending the last hour of your hunt think about what you'll say to whoever asks, "what did you see?" and coming up with two birds and a squirrel is boring.

At other times the hunt may be too interesting and you'll want to leave early because its very cold, or rainy, or whatever.

But leaving your stand before its time to do so is a terrible idea. The reason we pick specific times to enter and exit is because we want to move in before the deer and move out after the deer do. Moving before you should does nothing but scare deer that were not expecting you to be there.

No good can come from exiting early...unless you're the neighbor to whom an early exit scared the deer to.

Exiting your hunting stand is just as important as entering. Making noise while entering will cause the deer to leave before you hunt. And making noise after the hunt will keep the deer from returning.

The appropriate time to end a morning hunt is about an hour after you'd like to get out, several hours after if its cold out. That means at around nine or ten. Deer may return to their bedding areas later than you'd think.

The appropriate time to end an evening hunt is not whenever the law says you should (although you should unload and case your weapon at the appropriate time to be lawful), but about the time you can no longer see the sights on your weapon. Or maybe, a bit earlier if you are concerned about getting lost on the way out.

Worse than getting out early when there are no deer around (that you are aware of) is getting out when there are deer around you. Scaring deer is a good way to prevent them from returning. Scare even the does away and you'll scare the bucks away too.

I've waited more than an hour after dark to leave a stand while the deer are still around me. (With and unloaded weapon in order to meet the legal requirements.)

This is why it is best not to have your stand directly on top of food sources. Deer spend the night at their food sources and hunting over a big food plot, or field, in the evening may require that you wait until morning before they leave. Your stands should be between food and their bedding areas, not on top of them.

If the deer are late in leaving your area, you might have a friend drive his truck towards your stand to scare the deer. That way the deer will run from the lights and noise of a car instead of running from a person in a tree that they'll look out for in the future.

Leave your stand as stealthily as you entered.

41

Which deer should you shoot?

Deciding which sort of deer you should shoot should be done before you hunt.. You won't want any indecision when the time comes to take your shot either.

"If its brown, its down" means that you should hunt a lesser spot, but it is not as simple as shooting the first deer that you see. You'll not want to shoot a doe at your favorite stand, because all deer will want to avoid that place thereafter. While only hunting for meat you may very well shoot the first deer that you see, but it can pay to shoot a particular type of antlerless deer.

The older the doe is, the smarter the doe is. An old doe is wise to her environment and she'll not make it easy to shoot another deer around her. She won't let you get away with much in the way of sight sound or smell. A meat hunter should aim for that smart old doe that often notices hunters first.

Without an old doe around a meat hunter will often have the opportunity to shoot a young doe, doe fawn, or a buck fawn. The doe will be the biggest and the buck fawn will be the boldest.

Fawns are born in the spring and spend the next summer, fall, and winter with their mother. In the spring the doe will drive the buck fawn away. He'll be required to leave the area and find someplace where the does are unrelated to him to call his home. Doe fawns will stick with their mothers until or unless one dies or they are required to split up to find food.

So if you shoot the doe, the buck fawn won't be driven away and inbreeding is possible. A dead doe may also mean that the fawns are unable to survive on their own and shooting one deer could cause the deaths of three.

Shooting the buck fawn means that there will be one less buck around, likely for others miles away, to shoot. The first deer that I shot was a buck fawn, but I don't like the idea of shooting a deer before he can grow the antlers that I'm actually after.

Shooting the doe fawn means that there will be one less doe in your area. This will case bucks to spend more time elsewhere during the breeding season.

Meat hunters should, ideally, shoot smart old does first and after that focus on fawns.

Personally, I don't like shooting antlerless deer. Shooting bucks is great, but shooting does is like work; even if they're "big does." [insert eye roll]

When it comes to shooting bucks the quality of the deer in your area will determine the quality of bucks that you can shoot. The greatest hunter in the world cannot shoot a buck that isn't there. If you hunt a place where any buck is an accomplishment, then you should be happy when you shoot one, even if it isn't as big as those shot on TV.

Don't set your buck size limit higher than your hunting property can accommodate.

One of my outdoor goals every year is to shoot, at least, one buck every year. Because of the quality of the property and area that I deer hunt I can set my minimum size to a buck that is three and a half years old, or better. If I hunted a lesser property, or area, I'd need to adjust my minimum size downward, or accept that I wouldn't shoot a buck every year, or every three or ten years.

A beginning hunter should shoot the first buck that he can, for the experience, the satisfaction, and so on.

He should also shoot the second buck that he can, and maybe the third, fourth, fifth, sixth.... Shooting bucks is great, and the joy you get after shooting a deer will be greatest during the time that you are happy with shooting anything with horns. Hopefully you'll be happy shooting smaller bucks for a long while.

During this time you might very well shoot some nice bucks too. During my early hunting career I shot whatever buck came by, big or small.

At some point though you weill probably decide that you've shot enough small bucks (as if). Or you may hunt some place that has rules about the minimum size buck that you can shoot (In which case you have my sympathy). Even if there are minimum size rules where you hunt you should shoot the first buck or two that you can, and pay whatever fine, before letting the smaller bucks go.

Once its time to shoot bigger bucks you'll be looking to differentiate bucks by their age. Like I said in chapter four, a deer's age during hunting season is measured in years starting with one half of a years.

Most of the bucks that you shoot during your shoot-all-antlered-deer period will likely be bucks that are a year and a half old. When you decide to let smaller bucks go you'll want to plan on shooting a two and a half or better, and maybe several of them before deciding to push your size limit up another year.

Hopefully you'll be able to take my advice and shot lots of one and a half year old bucks. Once that is so, you should have at least seen a few older bucks, and you should have a better idea about estimating the age of the deer.

The younger the buck the longer they look and the pointer their noses look. The older bucks will look squarer and look like they have shorter noses. A deer, in Southern Wisconsin, should measure at around fifteen inches from ear tip to ear tip. A 2 ½ around here is likely to have an inside spread measurement of around fourteen inches. This may be of use in determining the age of the deer you see. Remember, however, that antler sizes are not a very accurate way to age a deer.

It was only when I started letting two and a half year old bucks go I could really tell the difference in body shape between 2 ½ and 3 ½. Before I started letting the 2 ½ go I just looked for my shooting opportunity at either age class buck rather than notice their differences.

Shoot some 1 ½ year old bucks, then shoot some 2 ½ and so on. They get harder to find and harder to kill the older they get, and by gradually increasing your minimum size you'll gradually

191

increase your skill level all while regularly shooting bucks that you are happy with.

There may be other factors that weigh into the size of the deer that you decide to shoot, such as the aforementioned local rules, the opinions of others (screw 'em), and the deer herd control practices in your area.

I say, forget about what anyone thinks of a deer that you shoot so long as you are happy with shooting it. Shoot the deer that you are happy to shoot.

The other hunters around you may want to let smaller bucks go, because dead deer get no bigger. This is good if that's what you want to do too.

Letting the smaller ones go means that more will grow and you'll likely see more big bucks because the smaller bucks usually arrive at your tree before bigger bucks do. Occasionally you may even see a line of bucks walk by your tree. When they do this they'll invariably start with the smallest and end with the biggest.

On January 1, 2010 I had six bucks walk in a line straight to me, each buck was a little bigger than the one before me. The smallest bucks don't come out first, but a bigger one won't always show up either.

(I didn't shoot a buck on January 1, 2010 because I was wearing a new coat which sounded like Velcro as I leaned away from my tree as I drew my bow. The moral of this story is that clothing and hunting equipment that makes noise are worse than worthless.)

As far as shooting bucks goes, deciding whether or not to shoot, as quickly as possible is what is most important. In our family, the guideline that we go by is that 'if you have to think about whether or not to shoot – don't shoot. But everyone makes their own decision on what a shooter for them is.

Before you hunt you should know approximately what you want to shoot. And when you see a buck you should glance at his antlers and think: yes or no. From that point on you should ignore the antlers. Only the direction of the eyes, ears, and the location of the chest should matter.

Spending too long looking at a buck's antlers is how you get "buck fever" (nervous/ exited to the point that you screw up your opportunity at a deer).

You can look at the antlers when the buck is dead.

I don't remember much about the seeing a bucks antlers before shooting them. I can tell you all about shooting them, what the deer did, where the shot hit the deer, and so on. But before the shot is made I glance at the antlers and think: yes or no.

Someone who misses a buck and who can tell you all sorts of intricacies and specific details about a deer's antlers spent too long looking at them and not enough time planning his shot. I've even heard of guys shooting through a buck's antlers rather than his chest because they were looking at antlers not their target.

Shoot what you like and compliment others on their deer. You'll want them to do the same for you. The golden rule is good, even if you think mean thoughts about hunter who shoot the buck you wanted to shoot. (The jerk.)

While the golden rule is grand for discussing the shooting of deer, for me personally, I'm uninterested in anyone else's deer. I try to pretend to be interested, to be polite, but I don't really care.

This would be different if one of you who reads this books takes this information and shoots a deer. In that case I'll get an ego boost for providing the information used to assist you in shooting your deer. I would be very interested to hear about deer shot by any of my readers. I'll also stick your picture on my blog if you want me to.

Unless you are friends/ family, or one of my readers I'm not interested in someone else's deer. Many people are motivated by their desire to do better than others. I'm happy when I shoot a deer, and less happy when I don't.

Don't worry about what the guys on TV and in magazines shoot. The more time you spend in good places the bigger the bucks you shoot will be.

42

When to Make Your Move

We now know what we want to shoot (a big buck, or maybe a medium one, small is good too).

When to shoot a deer, or when to make your move towards shooting a deer is critical in determining if you'll be successful.

This is one part of deer hunting that you'll foul up a lot. Lots and lots.

I'll compare my ability to kill a buck, once he's in range, with anybody. This is because I screwed up opportunities lots of times, and lots of different ways. Like everything else, you shouldn't make the same mistake twice. Make the mistake once and then learn from it.

The first thing is to be confident in your equipment and yourself. You should expect that once the deer gives you an opportunity the only thing to worry about is when, because you've practiced enough that the shot should be concern free. I practice shoot lots.

When you're seeing deer you need to be aware of your surroundings. You need to know where all of the nearby deer are, and you need to know where all of their eyes are pointing. You shouldn't smell, and you know your equipment won't make noise, so it's the deer's eyes that you'll be most concerned about when about to take the shot.

Obviously there's no point in moving when a deer is looking your way; you'd just scare all the deer before you can shoot. And even if all the deer are running all around and just happen to pause for a second in front of you, you want to move very, very slowly, or you'll scare the deer before you can shoot. (That's a 125B&C eight pointer I don't have.)

Slowly and quietly is good always.

So, you're in your stand and you've got the minimum size of the deer you want to shoot in your head. You will be looking and listening for signs of deer movement. You don't want to be halfway between sitting and standing, and you don't want to be turned into a position you can't stay in for a few minutes while a deer looks in your direction.

Just so we're clear: a deer looking in your direction means looking in the direction of the tree you are in, even if you are well above where you think the deer is looking. Movement just above where the deer is looking will catch his attention quite well.

At this point we've done all we can not to smell, and make noise, so we aren't concerned, at the moment, with being heard or smelled, but you should see where the deer's ears are pointing. A deer uses its ears to "see" behind, and around, it.

A deer's ears will usually be pointing in two different directions, and usually in a different direction from its nose and eyes. This gives the deer the ability to ne aware of noises all around it. When a deer is conscious of something but unsure of weather to be concerned about it, then the deer will point both of its ears and eyes at the point of interest for a few seconds.

When a nearby deer has both its ears pointed in the same direction, any direction, you cannot make any noise or move. That deer is at high alert.

When does think that something is around they have two tricks they will use to get whatever it is they are concerned with (usually you) to give away its position. These are two more situations when you absolutely cannot move or make any noise. When a buck is similarly concerned he'll just be gone.

Often a doe will look towards her point of concern and stomp a front foot in order to get you, or whatever, to move. She'll do this a few times, and then either walk away with glances over her shoulder, or ignore whatever it was she thought she heard. You don't want to move until you're sure she's over her concern.

The second "trick" a doe will use to detect her point of concern is to lower her head like she's going to eat something on

196

the ground. Then she will mover her head side to side, as if she is unaware of any danger and she'll appear as if she's looking for food. Then she'll jerk her head up quickly to try and catch the potential danger moving while it thought she was unaware.

If you see any number of does, you will see them do both of these "tricks" in order to help them locate any potential danger. Often she'll run about fifty yards away from where she was when she first became concerned stop their and look again towards her point of interest.

When you do scare does they'll often snort and make a whistle like noise to alert other deer. At this point you'll just need to wait for a few minutes before any action resumes.

"Spooking" does isn't good because your best opportunity to shoot bucks will occur when the bucks are following the does, and does avoid areas of danger.

The next thing to understand about when to make your move to shoot is to know that if a deer sounds like it is coming your way after another one, then it'll either be a group of does arriving independently, or if it's a line of bucks, then the biggest one will be the last one.

Bucks like to let does and smaller bucks into areas before they arrive so that any danger there can be detected by them and will befall them instead of him. Because of this when you sense a deer following another and coming your way, the second buck will usually be bigger than the first. One day I had six bucks walk right to me in single file, with each one a little bigger than the one ahead of him. And my new coat sounded like Velcro as I leaned away from the tree to shoot. (That's another 120 B&C buck I don't have.)

The positioning of the deer is important in planning your shot. With a rifle there are many more angles from which you can shoot a deer. With a rifle or a bow, the ideal of where you aim your shot will be to have the "quartering away" from you, and a broadside deer would be next best. A deer facing you or quartering on, even a little, is not shootable if you are bow hunting. (That's a 145 B&C buck I don't have.)

A "quartering away" deer is one that is not broadside, or facing straight on, but has its front further from you than its butt. This is the best angle for shooting, particularly with a bow because you can have your bullet or arrow get to the heart and lungs by going around, rather than through the shoulder/ front leg, as is necessary with deer that are broadside, or quartering on.

So, a deer you want to shoot is heading your way, you know the deer in the area are not aware of you, and you're ready to move to make your shot.

You'll want your gun's safety off or your lighted bow sight on (if you're using one) once you know the deer headed your way is one you want to shoot. Do that stuff if you're not sure of the deer's size yet, as there may not be any time for it later.

As you watch the deer approach you should be looking for where you think your shot will occur, when you make your move, and if you're using a bow you should take note of the range of your predicted shot. You're going to be thinking something like, "he's going to pass right past that tree, which is around twenty yards away, so I'll draw my bow when he passes that other tree." This planning will be very important when hunting in heavy cover and your planned shot needs to occur in a certain hole in the brush. Hitting obstructing brush is not good. (130 B&C)

You are going to want to take the first "good" shot opportunity that you get. When you see a deer that you do not want to shoot, it may be helpful to plan when you would make your move if you had wanted to shoot this deer.

After you let a few deer go you may be amazed at how many good shot opportunities that you get at deer after your first "good" one. You might think that you are only going to shoot when you have a perfect situation, but if you pass on your first good opportunity you may not get another one. Every second a deer you want to shoot is in your vicinity is another second of time in which he may detect your presence, or just wander off.

Once you've got planned your shot you should predict how long it will take him to reach that point. You cannot hold your gun up, or hold your bow drawn forever, you you'll want to raise your gun or draw your bow just before he reaches your planned shot.

Ideally you will raise your gun/ draw your bow when the deer in close enough for a shot and has his head behind a tree. This way you can move all you want and not be seen. Although some times you may try this and the deer will take one more step and stop with his head out from behind the tree and his "vitals," unshootably, behind that tree. (There are too many bucks to count that I don't have. When it works its perfect, when it doesn't...you can't hold your bow drawn forever.)

In practice you will make your move just before your first good shot opportunity, and you should have this moment planned before you need to do it.

Another thing to note is that deer are very good a disappearing. You may be watching a deer for a while and see him walk behind a tree. You may then look to the other side of the tree for a few minutes and not see him reappear. But then you may catch some movement out of the corner of your eye of that same deer dozens of yards from where you thought he should be. I don't know how a four foot long deer can disappear behind a tree with an eight inch diameter, but they do it surprisingly often. The solution to this problem is to keep your ears open and keep your eyes moving all around.

Don't focus your eyes on one place unless you can see a deer there. Keep your eyes moving or the deer you were looking at will reappear dozens of yards from where you thought he'd be.

You may try walking shots with a gun or a bow, but you are a lot more likely to miss them.

I've never wanted to alert a deer to my presence, but the thing to do with a walking deer is to make a noise that makes the deer stop and look your way, while you're aiming. "Hey." Making a noise can work but you will have only a second to shoot before the deer runs away.

A final suggestion is to remain still when a deer is going to walk past you, and then move once he passes you. Then you can turn around and shoot him from behind, when his attention is ahead of him. If you plan on doing this, and are wearing a safety harness, I recommend making sure that the tree strap is around the tree at your shoulder height while you are sitting. If you put that tree strap at waist height when you are sitting, you may not have enough strap to stand, turn, and shoot at the buck you just let pass. (That's a 115 B&C 8 point buck I don't have, and helped another guy put on his SUV a week later.)

In order to continue my list of failures, I'll point out that cheap ammo may misfire and cost you a deer. (125 B&C)

In 2011 I somehow missed a 150 B&C buck at like five yards with a rifle. And the next day I shot a ten pointer with a shot more difficult than I should have considered through brush I looked at later and could not see through.

Then there's the buck with the 18" spread that I shot in the guts with my bow, who proceeded to bed about seventy yards away for more than an hour and then got up and left, never to be seen again.

The second arrow I ever shot at a tree would have been great, if that 1" tree had not intercepted my arrow. The broadhead is still in that tree, which is now much bigger.

One Thanksgiving Day I missed a buck, and then dad's gun didn't fire because he eased his semi-auto bolt down rather than let it make noise and properly seat the cartridge.

Before I shot my first buck with a bow, I missed two, had one spook when I moved too soon, had my safety harness keep me from turning to shoot another, and missed another before the next buck that came by went down. Expect several foul-ups before being successful. If you avoid the mistakes that I mentioned in this chapter, then that should reduce the number of opportunities with bucks that you need in order to get one.

To summarize this chapter: First be aware of the focuses of attention for all the deer in your area. Second, identify the deer you want to shoot. Third, take safety off, or turn your lighted sight on. Fourth, plan your shot location and when you'll move. Fifth, make your move. Sixth, shoot. Seventh, follow the deer with your eyes and memorize where he goes to making trialing him, if necessary, easier.

43

Where to Shoot

There are lots of places you could shoot a deer and kill it.

You could shoot it in the head, and make a mess, and maybe damage the antlers, if you can even hit that small moving target.

You could shoot it in the neck, but there is more "air" in a neck than you'd think. Unless you hit the throat, spine, or correct veins you may just give it a flesh wound.

You could shoot it in the guts, and watch it run a long ways away, leave no blood trail, and have it die in lots of pain. (If you do shoot one in the guts, wait at least three hours before going after it, because it'll bed quickly and die there unless it's disturbed, in which case it'll run for miles.)

You could shoot a deer in the spine, and watch it be paralyzed from that point back.

Don't shoot it in the spine.

You could shoot a deer in the back leg, and hit the femoral artery, in which case it'll be down quickly, but you'll wonder how you hit it there. (If you see a dead buck with an arrow with two pink and one white feather sticking out of its back leg, then that would be mine. Two for two so far, and I don't know how I hit them there.)

You don't want to do any of that.

The best place to hit a deer is in the heart/ lungs area.

A heart shot, or hitting all the blood vessels just above the heart, is absolutely ideal. The deer will bleed a lot, and die quickly. The heart is located at the bottom of the deer's chest, just between its front legs. The buck I shot with my bow in 2012 had the exit hole at the bottom of the chest just behind the front leg. This was practically a drain hole for the heart and I had a foot wide solid blood trail for twenty yards. (Original Muzzy 3 blade broadhead, btw.)

Unfortunately the heart is a small target, and while you should be good enough to hit a target that size from whatever distance you are shooting, the bigger the room for error the better.

All this leaves us with the lungs as the ideal target. The lungs of a deer fill all of the chest where the heart isn't. So, about the front third of a deer's body is filled with the lungs. The front of the lungs will be covered by the deer's legs. Unless you hit a big bone, the legs are not too much of a problem for guns, but a leg shot with an arrow may only wound the deer.

The exact point you should aim for should be just along the back line of the front leg and between a third of the way up from the bottom of the chest, to about halfway between the top and bottom of the body.

Along the back line of the front leg, and halfway up to a third of the way up from the bottom.

Be sure to watch the deer for as long as possible after the shot, you want to make the blood trailing as easy as possible.

44

Blood Trailing

The most important part about finding a deer is shooting it well.

In any case, noticing where you hit the deer will be very important. A hit in the front of the chest may be in the leg, heart, lungs, or all the tubes coming out of the top of the heart. With a heart or lung shot you want to wait at least an hour before beginning to track it (okay, a half hour...try to wait as long as possible). A shot that hits the middle of the deer, you may notice its back "hump", will be a gut shot. A hit in the liver may leave lots of blood early, and then no blood for the rest of the 200 yards the deer will go before expiring.

A gut shot deer will run for a ways and then bed down to expire in an hour or two. With a gut shot deer you need to wait at least three or four hours. After a gut shot deer beds, it'll expire there if its not disturbed. If it gets disturbed, it'll get up and be gone (that's gone, like I hope he got his passport stamped when he crossed the border, gone).

With a bow:

- A heart shot deer will go twenty to thirty yards.
- A lung shot deer will go twenty to fifty yards.
- A liver shot deer will go two hundred yards.
- A gut shot deer will go a short distance and bed down, but if you jump him he will go for a long way.

Hit a deer anywhere else and you are not likely to recover the deer.

With a gun expect the deer to drop right there or run about the same distance as I just pointed out for bow shots.

First try to determine where the deer was hit on the follow through of your shot. Second, memorize where, exactly, the deer was when you shot and memorize where each rock, bush, tree he went past is. You'll need to find all of those things again on the ground, and it will be extremely difficult if you have no idea where he went especially as its likely to be after dark and getting late.

You may look for the arrow, or blood where the deer was when he was hit, before waiting for the deer to die, but go no further.

You will want to note what the any blood looks like: dark red blood means heart or liver, bubbly light red blood means lungs, non-red materiel means guts.

A flashlight after dark will be a great aid in blood trailing after dark, because wet blood will glisten in the light. The LED flashlights give a solid even white light that is the best light to look for blood. The standard, inconsistently bright yellow lights, and blood specific lights are much inferior to LED flashlights.

While trailing the deer lift your feet, do not kick around leaves that may have blood on them.

If there's no blood, then follow the stirred up leaves.

Understand that if the deer does not drop inside 100 yards, you are likely going to need patience, diligence and maybe some luck to find it. Your last option is to walk in concentric circles around where you last saw the deer. Always check the thickest cover in the area, and always check any areas where there is water. A gut shot deer will very often go to water if it can make it that far. So check ditches, water holes, creek or river bottoms and lake and pond edges. Don't give up.

If you don't find it, listen for crows, or other animals, the next few days, they may have found it first. If it is warm go back out and see if you can find it by smell.

The last thing to keep in mind about blood trailing is that this is the only time you should ever walk into your deer bedding areas.

You owe it to the deer to make all the effort that you can in order to find it.

45

Field Dressing

Field dressing is the removal of the internal organs from a dead deer. You want to remove the organs quickly because doing so will cool the deer more quickly. The faster the meat is cooled the better the meat will be.

Even if you plan on taking the deer to a professional, or friend, to do the butchering you'll need to do the field dressing yourself.

The equipment for removing the organs is a study knife and field dressing gloves. The disposable orange gloves will cost less than $2 at your sporting goods store. Look for the gloves that also contain the white surgical gloves which will keep the big orange ones tight to your hands.

You can forgo the gloves if you want, but you'll spend how long covered in blood afterwords? Will you clean your truck's steering wheel and door handles, etc. after you've covered them with blood?

I like fixed blade knives better than folders.

First drag the deer to wherever you want its organs to end up. It doesn't seem to matter much, but I prefer to leave gut piles where I park my car rather than where I expect the deer to be.

Remove your coat and some top layers of clothing to be more maneuverable, and get fewer clothing items bloody. Then you'll put the long, past elbow gloves on, and then the surgical gloves over your hands.

Roll the deer onto its back. It will want to roll to one side. If someone else is around, get them to hold one side's legs to keep the deer upside down. If no one is around, hold a leg with a leg of yours to keep it upside down.

You'll want to stand behind the deer to start, with its head away from you.

Keep the knife blade up because you do not want to puncture the organs, especially if you found the deer the morning after you shot it (more smell).

Stick the knife in shallowly, blade up, pointing forwards in the middle of the belly. Cut the skin to the middle of the bottom of the rib cage. The ribs will form a V. You can feel this point on yourself. Notice where your abs are soft (or rock hard in my case) and feel up your middle until you hit the rib intersection.

Connecting both sides of the ribs is a bone called the sternum. Your cut will need to go to the neck, but you'll be unable to cut through the sternum. Cut the cartilage and ribs along one side of the sternum all the way up to the base of the neck. The deer's left side works for me because I'm right handed, but it doesn't matter which side.

Then turn your knife around and cut the skin to the reproductive organs. You'll want to cut all the way around them. The male's will be easy to identify and the female's udder will be detectable too.

Cut around the genitals and then cut the tube connecting them. You may want to tie off the tube with string, because that tube if full of things you'll not want to contaminate your meat with.

Then I expect that you'll throw the deer's dick at whoever happens to be around. They always like that.

You'll need to cut all the way to, and around, the anus as well. This tube you'll definitely want to tie off; you do not want its contents to mix with the meat you will eat.

You might get a small saw just to spit the pelvic bone. There will be a little part of that bone that goes over the tube of excrement. In stead of cutting the bone to remove the tube, you can buy a "Butt Out" and pull the tube out and then cut and remove it.

Now turn your attention to the middle of the deer. The diaphragm is a membrane that is perpendicular to the rest of the

207

deer; it goes around the middle, at the back of the rib cage. You'll want to cut the diaphragm and whatever else connects the organs to the spine and ribs.

Then you'll need to go into the rib cage and remove the heart, lungs, and as much of the esophagus as you can get. This will include cutting most of the diaphragm away. All other cuts should be at the base of the neck and alongside the insides of the ribs.

Cut, cut, cut, then roll the deer to one side and pull all of the organs out.

Some people save the heart and liver to eat; I do not.

Then you should roll the deer right side up to drain the blood that will have pooled. A fine way to drain the blood, and make the deer pose for pictures, is to spread each leg out a different way. This will leave the stomach cavity pointing down to drain the blood, and the deer's head will be "sitting" on its shoulders in a fine position for picture taking.

Next you'll want to drag the deer to wherever you want to take pictures, and then take them. (Picture taking will be covered in another chapter.)

Once your deer is field dressed and you've taken pictures you'll either take the deer to a meat processor to do the butchering for you, or to wherever you are going to butcher it yourself.

Personally I usually take my deer in to be processed, this will cost a couple hundred bucks, depending on what you want done: sausage, steaks, jerky, etc.

Field dressing may well be considered the grossest part about deer hunting. It is something that needs to be done. Even if you'd rather not do it, and even if you are going to have someone else do the butchering, you need to field dress your deer. Its not as bad as you may think it is. If you don't like this part, then I recommend re-reading this chapter before you go hunting and have the things that you need to do memorized. Once the tasks are memorized, you can forget about doing it, so long as you remember how.

After you've field dressed one or two you'll never think about it again. Its just a job that needs to be done. If your son is hunting, have him take care of his first deer, with your instruction, so that ever after he need not be concerned with thinking about it. Get the first one over with and never worry about it again.

46

Skinning and Butchering

I do not have a whole lot of experience butchering deer myself, so you may want to look elsewhere for more, or better, information. But here is what I know:

The faster you cool the meat the tenderer it will be. The longer you wait after it is killed to cool the meat, the tougher it will be.

Equipment needed for butchering is: a sharp knife, containers for the meat, rope to hang the deer, rubber gloves, a meat saw, and maybe a gambrel to assist the deer hanging.

First find a horizontal branch or beam to hang the deer from. My grandfather knew when a buck he shot was big when its nose touched the floor of his garage when it hung from a garage rafter. This branch, or rafter, should be sturdy.

You might have a gambrel, which looks like a heavy duty metal coat hanger with a hook on each end. If you have a gambrel, you'll cut a hole in the skin of each back leg. This hole will be at the middle leg joint. You'll only need to cut a bit of skin there at the joint, it should be an obvious spot. Stick a gambrel hook through each hole and then hang it from your branch.

If you don't have a gambrel, you'll use some rope tied to each leg and over the branch. You'll want the legs to be tied a ways apart so you'll have minimal twisting while you work.

Having another person hold a leg will keep the deer from twisting too.

The first task is skinning.

Just below (as it hangs) the joint in the back leg the leg will widen. You'll want to cut the skin around both legs there. Then you'll want to cut a straight line through the skin from your first cuts, down the inside of the legs and to the field dressing cut in the middle of the bottom of the deer.

Then, mostly, you'll pull the skin down off of the legs. You may use the knife to speed the skin removal, but the pulling should do most of the work. It will be a slow hard pull.

After the legs have been skinned you'll continue down the body. And then make similar front leg cuts as you did on the back legs.

The skin will be pulled off the body just like it was pulled off the legs.

If you are going to have your deer mounted you'll skin to just past the front shoulders and then cut the neck and head off just above the shoulders. You'll leave the skin, head, and neck, together for your taxidermist. Take it to him quickly before it goes bad. Refrigerate if you must delay taking it to your taxidermist.

If you are not going to have the deer mounted you'll want to maximize the amount of skin in one piece until just below the head, and then cut around the neck below the head. And then one more cut down the center of the bottom of the neck, from head to chest, will be your last skinning cut.

Then you'll roll the skin up. Ideally you will cover the meat side of the skin with a thick layer of salt. And then you can take the skin to a tannery.

A dedicated meat saw will be the means of head removal. If you're skillful, you may cut, with the knife, between the vertebrae to remove the head.

You may want to switch knives at this point when you begin to butcher.

I would like to take this time to point out that I'm not as skilled as I might be at butchering deer. But the following should get you started.

You'll need a knife and plastic bag or containers into which you'll put the meat, a cooler, or freezer, freezer paper, and perhaps another knife.

A perk of butchering deer yourself is that some meat processors use saw for some cuts, and saws will get some bone dust mixed with the meat. Using knives only should improve the taste.

A skinned hanging deer, or pig or cow I would imagine, looks just like so much meat and not so much like a deer.

Along the spine and the tops of the legs are best. The neck and between the ribs will be of lesser quality.

Deer meat is different from beef or pork, less fatty and more protein, so look up venison specific recipes, or your venison in beef recipes will go badly.

Picture Taking

There are two ways to take your own trophy deer pictures. One way is to have lots of trail cameras in areas where there are trophy bucks, and the other is to shoot big bucks and then take pictures of them.

Covert   10.19.2012 03:51:40

There are some tips that will improve your chances of getting those big pictures.

The first "trick" to getting big deer pictures with a trail camera is to have a lot of cameras and put them where lots of big deer live. If there are no big deer you won't get pictures of them.

When you put trail cameras up on your property you should take care with how you get the cameras out, and where you put them. If your cameras smell like gas, or you, or any other human smell, then the deer, especially big deer, will avoid the cameras. If you have a deer sanctuary, that means never entering it, even for pictures.

One thing I am guilty of, especially during the summer, is to not take as much care while going in to check the camera and collect the memory cards. When I go hunting I cautiously walk in as silently and as un-noticeably as possible. When I am at the property checking trail cameras, I haven't been as good about avoiding smells and I am less interested in moving as stealthily as I should be.

Take some time to think about where you put your trail cameras. If you want to cover a trail, then don't put the camera on the trail you should have it a few feet away. Think like you would if you were standing and taking the picture yourself.

Also consider putting the camera higher up trees. Deer may not notice a camera 6-8 feet up a tree. Deer, and people, spend our days looking straight ahead and down, an little time looking up. How often to you look at you ceiling?

Modern digital trail cameras have batteries and memory cards that can take thousands of pictures with no input from you. You don't need to check your cameras every week. When we still used film trail cameras, I checked one every week. The first week at this camera had 15 different bucks, between 1 1/2 and 3 1/2 years old. The second week had like 6 different bucks on it, and the third week had 2 or 3 small bucks only. Check your cameras only when you need to.

The biggest trick in getting trophy deer pictures is having lots and lots of pictures to sort through and find those few pictures of big bucks.

A good way to get a good picture of a big buck is to shoot a big buck.

With lots of pictures I have lots of choices to pick the ones I like best.

Good pictures make your deer look bigger. There is not as much as you can do with smaller bucks, but if you shoot a great big buck, then you will want to be prepared for taking the best pictures possible.

The second trick to having your deer look bigger in pictures is to take lots of different pictures from different angles and locations and positions.

Turn the deer's head in different ways. Take pictures from the deer's right and left, front and back. Take pictures with the deer on the ground, take pictures with the deer in the back of your truck, etc. You don't know which pictures will be the best. A slight angle can make a big difference and you won't know which angle is best until you review the pictures.

Don't waste your time looking at the pictures as you take them. Even though you can use a digital camera to see pictures after you've taken them, you should just take lots of pictures and review them later.

A lot of hunters use head-on shots for their perspective, and this is not the best angle from which to view a buck; you can't see the sides if you look straight on. Bucks often look better from behind, and I make a point of getting a picture from behind of the bigger deer I shoot.

Another thing to do is to use more than one camera. I don't have a picture of a 51″ muskie because of a camera malfunction which was not noticed until after the fish was released. If you want to be sure of a good picture, buy a disposable film camera to supplement your digital one, in case you shoot a big buck.

If I shoot a big buck, I will remove my legally required orange and camouflage before the pictures. A solid color background for the antlers will be better than the camouflage we are wearing when we shoot.   And orange is no one's color, not even a deer's.

50

Antler Removal

For some of us acquiring deer antlers are a goal of hunting. Once you have shot your buck you have a few options on how to remove the antlers.

First decide if you are going to mount the deer antlers. If you are you need to leave the cape (skin) in tact well past the head. For the usual head mount this means keeping the skin whole, past the shoulders. Talk to your taxidermist, before you take care of your antlers and skin. (If you drop your deer off at a meat shop that processes game animals they can take care of this too.)

You need two tools and ideally a helper to hold the antlers and keep them from moving while you cut. The tools are: any old knife (preferably sharp) and a meat saw.

If you take your deer to a meat shop cut the antlers off yourself. You'll be able to do it exactly how you want it.

One more thing to keep in mind is that it is better to do this right away it gets more difficult, and gross, the longer you wait.

You have 3 options for separating the deer antlers from the rest of the deer: the fast and traditional option, a below the ears option, and a full skull "European mount" option.

For every option, cut with the knife to the bone and then use the saw.

1. The fastest, perhaps traditional, option is to make a cut in front of and a cut behind the base of the antlers, and have them meet in the middle.

This will leave you with the barest minimum skull necessary to keep the antlers together. This is not much, and I'd bet easy to break. If your buck is going to be mounted this is what the taxidermist will do. The foam that makes the deer shape inside of the mount has an opening to fit this cut.

My preferred option for antler removal is to cut below the ears, through the bottom of the eye, and out between the eyes and nose.

I like this the best because I am still left with much of the top of the skull which is more bone to keep the antlers together. I've tried and there is NO way to cut the horns off above the ears which leaves you with any amount of skull behind the horns.

A second, and vertical cut is sometimes necessary in order to get the brain out, and to remove the a difficult to remove meat from the back of the skull.

The last option is to keep a full skull, perhaps for a European mount. To do this: cut, with a knife, all of the skin and meat off. And then you'll need to do a thorough job of removing all of the little bits of meat.

No matter how you remove the antlers from the deer removing all of the smallest bits of meat can be done by either boiling the skull, but not the horns, in a big pot of water or by giving the antlers to a taxidermist who has the flesh eating beetles eat the meat off for you.

49
Antler Scoring

Once you've shot your buck and removed the antlers you may be interested in scoring the antlers, for a variety of reasons.

If your antlers are big enough you can get them included in Boone & Crockett's world record book, or in Pope and Young's record book, or some other record book. Keep in mind that there are minimum size requirements, and all sorts of other requirements in order to be included in one of those record books. For detailed, and up to date, information on all of those rules and requirements check out their websites.

For the most part there are two varieties of whitetail deer antlers, typical and non-typical. Typical antlers are shaped in the basic way, with main beams leaving the head and going up, out, then forwards, and the rest of the tines will go straight up from the main beams.

Non-typical whitetail deer antlers will be those that do anything other than that. With the B&C scoring system their definition of non-typical is a certain percentage of the antlers being abnormal.

In order to be accepted into the record book you'll need to hit the minimum size, have it scored by accepted experts, wait for the drying period to end, and so on. But a rough estimation of your deer's antlers will give you an idea of how big your buck is, give you perspective on how big other deer that you see are, and will let you know if your buck is big enough to be scored by a B&C approved scorer.

The tools that you will need in order to score your antlers are: a writing instrument, paper, maybe a calculator, and a soft tape measure. A soft tape measure is usually used in sewing, and you can buy one for a dollar or two anywhere that sells sewing things. If you do not have a soft tape measure, then you'll want to cut about three feet of string and hold the marked string to a yardstick for measurements.

On the paper you'll want a chart with four columns and many rows. The first column will be the names of the rows, the second column will be for left side measurements, the third column for right side measurements, and the fourth is for the differences between the two. The rows will be named: "Main beam," "G-1," "G-2," "G-3," "G-4," "G-5," "H-1," "H-2," "H-3," "H-4," and the final row will be the inside spread. (The "tip-to-tip spread" of the deer's antlers is included in all of the B&C charts, but that number is ignored in the final score.)

All measurements are to the nearest 1/8 of an inch.

First measure along the outside of one main beam from the ridge around the base of the antler next to the head, this is known as the "pedicle." Put the number in the chart under "left", "main beam." Do the same for the other side.

Next you'll measure the length of the first point above the antler base, this is the "G-1." Measure from where the tine separates from the main beam to its tip. This point, or tine, is often missing on smaller bucks and either missing or only an inch long on mule deer. The G-1 is often called a "brow tine." Both sides are to be done again.

You'll work your way up from the base of the beam, and out until you run out of tines, G-2, G-3...

After the tines are measured for both sides, you'll want to measure the circumferences of the beams. The first circumference is between the pedicle and the G-1. The second circumference is between the G-1 and G-2. And so on.

The first measurement is the "H-1" measurement. You get as many "G" measurements as you have typical points but you only get four "H" measurements.

Next you'll get the measurement from inside the main beams, from beam to beam, this is the "inside spread".

Finally, if you have any points that are "non-typical," then they will be measured, for length, and added up, and then entered

219

as one number. No two measurers will get the same score for any buck, let alone, a non-typical one.

Your fourth column will be the differences between the two sides. If your left main beam is 23 inches and the right main beam is 24 inches then you'll put a "1" in the fourth column. Then do the same for all of the "G" and "H" measurements.

Add the numbers or the left side, and write it under the left side. Then add the numbers for the right side and write it under the right side's numbers. And add the numbers in the differences column.

Your buck's "gross score," and the number most reflective of its size, is the sum of the left side total, the right side total, and the inside spread. For non-typicals you will add the non-typical total.

The score that may enter your buck into the record book will be its "net score." In order to get its net score you will add the left and right side totals, subtract the differences totals, and then add the inside spread. And for non-typicals you'll then add the non-typical total.

Just so you know, the world record typical whitetail scores around 216, and the world record non-typical scores around 336.

With this chapter I expect that you now know how to approximate your deer's antler's score and you'll be able to know if your buck is big enough to get scored by the experts, and you now know what I mean when I say something like "143 inch ten" (143 gross B&C score, ten points).

50

Hunting Successes (and Failures)

My First Buck

When I was thirteen I started more to seriously deer hunt, than I did when I was 12 and I shot a buck fawn the same day as my dad shot a 18" 10. During the early archery season I saw a few bucks, missed two, and missed a few other opportunities. My grandfather ended his lifetime of hunting two years prior and I inherited his spot.

On opening day of the gun deer season, the most important day of the year, I was ready and up a tree next to my grandfather's longtime ground blind.

A half hour, or so, after dawn I had a 1 1/2 old 8 pointer follow a doe to my right. I shot and watched the buck run away. I shot again and the buck walked away. I could have shot again but I thought that if I had missed twice already, then there was no point in missing again.

After a few hours my dad, who had heard my shooting, came over to see what the deal was. When I told him that the buck had walked away after my second shot he thought that I must have hit it or the buck would have ran away.

We followed the deer's trail for a few hundred yards. And when my dad talked to a neighbor hunter, I discovered the skull of a long dead 3 1/2 year old buck. The skull and horns were white and crumbly. They were also chewed through by squirrels (there are minerals in antlers and bones).

When my dad came back, he was looking at the skull and horns, while I held both rifles. While holding the two rifles, another buck appeared a few dozen feet away. I attempted to give my dad back his rifle so that I could shoot with mine. But by the time I had only one rifle the buck had disappeared.

My dad returned to his stand and I to my grandfather's ground blind, feeling rather poorly. Not a half hour later a saw a deer with a flash of white above the head. I shot as soon as possible.

It turned out to be a spike. 9 1/2 inches on the right and a busted off 4 inches on the left.

I made a series of mistakes, but I shot a buck. It was a good day.

My 2012 Archery Season

I attempted to shoot two bucks with my bow this past season. I missed one and got one. You may be able to learn from the stories of my two shots at deer with a bow this year (2012).

Let's start with the deer story that includes a happy ending.

I picked a new treestand location this year because I wanted a stand closer to the cover than I had in previous years. I picked a tree that covered a corner of brush and trees. If deer move from the main bedding area to my big food plot, then they will pass through this corner of brush and trees.

I probably averaged seeing three 1 1/2 year old bucks each night that I sat there. So one night I first saw the standard nine does and fawns and the usual two 1 1/2 year old bucks. Then in the distance I saw another deer and a flash of some long tines over its head. I saw parts of the deer for a time straight ahead of me through lots of brush and branches. He was following a doe and I expected him to pass by me.

His tine length meant that I knew that I wanted to shoot him if I got an opportunity. He took his time walking around about 30 yards in front of me, but there were too many branches to shoot through.

I expected him to walk from in front of me to my right. While I was waiting for him to clear the brush I considered which sight pin I would use. (Bow sights often have 3 or 5 pins. You put the top pin on a target that is 20 yards away, the second on a target that is 30 yards away, etc.) I thought that if he cleared the brush at one point that he would be twenty yards away. If he cleared the brush near some taller grass, then I'd use the 30 yard pin...

And then I realized that I was thinking too much. I've shot several deer, I've shot my bow a lot. So, I stopped thinking, and when the deer presented me with a shot, I lifted my bow and shot him.

I don't remember raising my bow, I don't remember putting the sight on the deer...I just did it.

Once you have shot your bow enough and become confident that you will be successful when shooting at deer, then you to will no need to over think taking a shot.

I hit him a bit far back, but he was quartering away and the exit hole was right behind the right front leg. This hole acted as a drain of the heart and I had a foot wide, solid blood trail for about 20 yards until I found the dead buck. (picture in chapter 30)

Now that you know what to do, let's look at what not to do.

Another night I was in the same tree and saw the usual few does, fawns, and small bucks. Then a deer came from behind me ant to my right. I got a glimpse of him through a clearing, and I would have had a shot if he had given me a bit more warning before showing up.

He looked big, but I did not know how big. I heard him rub his head in some branches over a scrape, but I could not see him because a tree was between us. He looked like a nice one. But how big?

"HOLY SHIT!"

223

My guess was that his gross B&C score was in the 170's, but I recently learned that a neighbor shot one that year that scored 192.. And I have a few trail camera pictures from nearby of a buck about that big at around the same time.

I had a great look at his antlers through some tree branches, but no shot.

"I can shoot through those branches," I thought. "No, he's following that doe. He's about to give me a good shot...But I can shoot through those branches...I shouldn't. How big are his...freaking huge...don't look at the horns wait for the shot...please move, please move, please move...he's a monster...don't look at the horns; wait for a shot."

And after a while he took a few steps out from behind the tree and presented me with a picture perfect 12 yard, standing, broadside, shot.

At this point I'd like to point out the two types of releases. One type of release has a metal buckle, like your belt, and the other uses Velcro to attach to your wrist. I prefer the Velcro because there is no metal to click against anything and make a noise. The problem with my Velcro was the tag end. I did not need the full length of Velcro to attach the release to my wrist.

And I was wearing a plastic mesh face-mask, to be more camouflaged.

Once I had the shot: I drew my bow, and my release's tag end made a ripping noise as it brushed against my face-mask.

When that happened all that I could think of was that I had made a noise, buck, heard it, and was about to run away.

"Shoot! Shoot! Shoot!" Was all that I could think.

I panicked, rushed my shot, and missed by a mile.

Dammit.

(For all of you who think that I would not have had this problem with buckled release strap, I'd like to point out that a buckle has metal parts which also make noise, and are actually much more likely to make noise when they hit anything. And that strap's tag end has been removed and trashed since.)

Conclusion

And so we end my first book. I think that I have covered all of the basics and equipment that you need to get started in hunting whitetail deer. There are, of course, more advanced ideas and things that you can do, but the preceding should be your fundamentals.

Find a good spot. Hunt there a lot. Hit what you aim at. Don't make the same mistake twice.

These are the points to remember.

I spend most every weekend from when the snow starts to melt in March through the end of the deer season in early January either hunting or improving my property. There are always things to be done.